D1569075

TRAINING YOUR
OWN YOUNG HORSE

TRAINING YOUR OWN YOUNG HORSE

Jan Dickerson

DOUBLEDAY & COMPANY, INC.
GARDEN CITY, NEW YORK
1978

Library of Congress Cataloging in Publication Data

Dickerson, Jan.
    Training your own young horse.

    1. Horse-training.   I. Title.
SF287.D53   636.1'08'88
ISBN 0-385-02222-0
Library of Congress Catalog Card Number 74–9444

To Marty and Clyde Nichols
AND TO
Kansas City

Contents

Preface

If the training of horses required solely an ability to "show 'em who's boss" by physical domination, I would have lost interest in it years ago. I would find no satisfaction in an endeavor that exercised the muscles but not the mind, and drew on courage but not on sensitivity. As it is, the training of horses involves body and mind and spirit, a fact which should become apparent to any serious reader of this book.

The first three chapters of the book are introductory, intended to give the novice trainer an insight into the psychology of horses. The remaining chapters are concerned with the basic training of the young horse. The assumption is that you have a young horse that you want to "break in" to riding. The chapters are arranged in a progressive sequence, and should be read and applied in the order that they are presented.

Glance at the Table of Contents, and you will note, perhaps to your surprise, that there is much training to be done before you mount your horse for the first time. You won't even need a saddle until you have worked your way into Chapter IX! You may wonder why you should bother with such details as sacking, longeing and line-driving before you start riding your horse, especially if you happen to have a colt that is big enough to ride, and already gentle enough to allow you to sit on his back. There are two reasons why you should "bother" with the preliminaries of ground schooling: 1. The more your young horse knows of discipline and work before he is ridden, the more quickly and surely he will learn his early lessons under saddle. 2. The more *you* know of the techniques of teaching a young horse to behave well and work under your direction while dismounted, the more ably you will handle the problems that arise when you are riding him.

You can be sure that there will be problems in the training of your horse, both during ground schooling and during mounted work, because that is what training is all about. As a trainer, you will be *creating* problem situations whenever you ask your horse to do something that he either does not understand or does not want to do. Your job is to resolve these problems in your own favor by helping the horse understand what you want of him, and by instilling in him an attitude of willing obedience.

Above all else, the goal of the intelligent and sensitive trainer is to teach his horse to work for him willingly and confidently. Although you may have heard that horses are "honest" or "dishonest" by nature, the plain truth is that horses acquire their attitudes in the course of their training. If you have a horse that has never been handled by anyone else, and he turns out to be a trustworthy and dependable mount under your training, it will be because you have made him so. If your horse already has been handled, and has developed a sour attitude because of poor training, your every effort should be directed toward changing that attitude. I hope that you will be successful, but don't consider yourself a failure as a trainer if you cannot effect a total reform. Young horses usually are more responsive to retraining than older horses; however, sometimes what has been done to them cannot be undone.

How can a young horse be taught an attitude of willingness? Not by subjecting him to the simpleminded "show 'em who's boss" approach to training, which consists of reaching for a whip every time the horse fails to do what is expected of him. That approach is based on the notion that whenever a horse misbehaves he is guilty of deliberate disobedience. It makes no allowances for the very likely possibility that the horse does not understand what he is supposed to do, or that he is afraid to do it. If you want your horse to develop a good attitude, then you must learn to interpret his behavior so that you can act in a way that will gain his confidence. It is a mistake to punish a horse when he is confused or afraid. Conversely, it is a mistake *not* to punish him for deliberate disobedience.

What is being said here is that it is only through learning to understand the behavior of a horse *in depth* that you can learn to manage his behavior. That is the real challenge and the fascination of horsemanship. It is my earnest hope that this book will excite your interest in that challenge, and will help you to give your young horse the kind of basic training that will prepare him to fulfill those dreams you have for his future.

JAN DICKERSON

TRAINING YOUR
OWN YOUNG HORSE

CHAPTER I

Your Role as a Trainer

Rodeo stock dealers say that some of the best broncs that come into their hands are not wild horses but saddle horses that have been spoiled into bucking by novice owners and trainers. The spoiled horses can be relied upon as rodeo performers, because in their "breaking" at home they were either coddled or bullied into meanness, and they learned the one lesson that ordinary saddle horses never should learn—that they are bigger and stronger than people.

Fortunately, not all horses handled and started under saddle by novice trainers turn into bucking broncs. Far too many of them, however, are allowed or unintentionally goaded into the development of tricks of behavior that range from annoying to frustrating to dangerous. Uncontrollable prancing, for instance, can be extremely annoying to a rider. Balking, whether it is a flat refusal to go forward, or a subtle but deliberate quitting of effort under stress, is frustrating. A habit of rearing, bolting, or violent shying is downright dangerous.

Bad habits, particularly those which enable horses to render their riders temporarily helpless, are difficult and sometimes impossible to "cure." Skilled trainers may overcome them, to the extent that *they* can control difficult horses, but they cannot guarantee that they have erased the undesired traits and that they will not reappear quickly under less-than-expert riders. It is for this reason that professional horse trainers usually find it far more to their preference to work with colts that have had no handling at all than to try to reclaim those that have been taught to be problems.

It seems important to make this point about bad habits at the outset of a book on the subject of training young horses, especially for those readers who may not fully realize that training is a two-sided task. It should be obvious that training involves teaching a horse *good* habits of performance. It may not be so obvious that an even greater challenge in early schooling is in seeing to it that a horse does not learn *bad* habits. The best trainers are ever alert to note the first small signs of problem behavior in young horses and are swift to take corrective action. Poor trainers lack the knowledge to see trouble coming, and the skill to forestall it.

It is not always the novice trainer who makes the mistake of thinking that training is a one-sided task. There are self-styled horsemen in the professional ranks who specialize in starting young horses but accept no responsibility for the bad habits their charges develop. In their ignorance they honestly believe that horses turn into problems only because they are "born that way." An example is a part-time trainer in a Western state who always warns his customers not to expect miracles. "Breaking young horses is a gamble, and a poor one at that," he says. "I know, because I've started many colts, and very few have turned out to be any good!"

Do all horses have a tendency to develop bad habits during training? The answer, without qualification, is that they do, even when they are treated lovingly and given the best of everything. This may come as a disappointment to some readers, who cannot see why a horse would repay kindness with misbehavior, but there is an explanation for it. Horses are born with no "habits" at all, and with no sense of right and wrong. They do have a strong sense of self-preservation, which means they are interested in their own welfare. In the process of their training to become useful saddle mounts, there are many moments when they feel threatened, and there are times when they feel uncomfortable. They feel threatened when they do not understand new lessons. They feel uncomfortable when they are tired, or when bits or saddles or clumsy riders cause them pain. It is natural for them to experiment with tactics to find relief from fear and discomfort, and if their experimenting is rewarded with success, then bad habits are on the way.

Taming vs. Training

Although it was stated earlier that it should be obvious that training involves teaching a horse *good* habits of performance, even this is not clear to some novice horsemen. Some novices, particularly those who have storybook ideas about horses, think "taming" is the same as "training." They think that, once a horse is gentle, he will somehow know what is expected of him. Mild-natured persons are sure that love and kindness will make a young horse tame, and often they do. Aggressive persons think the secret is in "showing the horse who's boss," and their method of "bucking a colt out" also may tame a horse. But neither method produces a *trained* horse. To tame a horse, one need only teach him to accept the presence of human beings. To train a horse, a person must be able to teach the horse to understand and habitually obey certain signals. There's a big, big difference.

It is a curious fact that people in general have only the dimmest notion of the difference between taming and training animals. Consider, for instance, a person who has a pet dog that won't come when it is called. When that person sees a dog that is well trained in obedience, he invariably exclaims about its intelligence. "That's one of the smartest dogs I have ever seen," he may say. It does not occur to him that the dog may have less intelligence than his own spoiled pet, and that the "smartness" is not in the dog, but in the trainer. The same is true of owners of poorly trained horses. They watch an expert trainer work with a colt and see the colt progress rapidly, and instead of appreciating the artistry of the trainer, they congratulate him on his "luck" in finding such a "well-behaved" and "smart" colt.

This is not to say, in reference to horses, that some are not more talented than others in learning certain skills. Some horses are built to be great jumpers; some are alert, quick and surefooted enough to be champion cutting horses; some are the "fantastic movers" that dressage trainers love to find. But it *is* to say that talent is only realized through training. Good training can make an average horse perform well. Poor training can blot out the abilities of a talented horse.

This is the significant thing to remember: It is not in the *taming* but in the *training* that many novices ruin their horses. Almost any sweet young girl can enjoy the thrill of taming a skittish colt so that it will come running to her for a cube of sugar. Given enough time, she can even cajole it into allowing her to sit on its back without any fuss. And an athletic youth with a yen for it can become a "horse breaker," specializing in climbing on colts and "bucking them out." But whether the same girl and boy (or a woman or a man) can *train* horses to *work* for them, doing willingly whatever they are supposed to do, is another matter entirely.

Plainly it takes more than love and/or courage to be a horse trainer. It takes the ability to 1. explain to a horse what is expected of him, and 2. require him to do it. And, if a trainer wants a young horse to develop a happy and not a sour attitude, it takes the ability to detect and thwart misbehavior before it leads to a bitter contest of wills. These abilities are not inborn in anyone. They are *acquired skills*.

The Timid and the Bold

It is perhaps too much a generalization to say there are two kinds of novice trainers, the gentle (usually women) and the aggressive (usually men), for gentle persons often have aggressive traits, and vice versa. But it does seem to be a fact that beginning trainers either are too gentle or too aggressive.

Gentle beginners tend to be patient to a fault, to such an extent that their "patience" actually becomes permissiveness. They tend to want to avoid trouble, because meeting trouble requires positive action, and for one reason or another they are afraid to try to assert themselves. They may say they don't want to be "mean" to their horses, when the truth is that they are afraid their horses will be mean to them. As trainers they are wishful thinkers, not doers. Their horses develop an "I don't even want to try and you can't make me" attitude about many things. It is interesting to note, however, that although their horses turn out to be nasty characters they usually are cool about it—their bucking, rearing, or balking is calculated more to threaten than to injure, and it stops as soon as they win their point. They may be quite agreeable about doing other things.

Aggressive beginners tend to be impatient. When their horses fail to obey them they are too ready to assume that the horses "know better," when in fact they may not. When trouble occurs they, no less than their too gentle counterparts, may be frightened, but instead of giving up they overreact. In other words, when they don't know what else to do, they resort to force. Their "training" sometimes produces gruesome results. Their horses may turn out to be vicious, or they may be given to frenetic behavior, or they may simply become lifeless, dispirited hulks.

It is wrong to assume that being too gentle is less a fault than being too aggressive, even though it would appear that the horse suffers less in the hands of a timid trainer. In the long run the horse that is babied into bad habits has to pay dearly for his misbehavior. Eventually his owner will be so frustrated or frightened that he either will try to correct the faults or will send the horse to a professional trainer to be corrected. Whoever tries to correct the faults will have to be very tough about it, and very sure, and even then may not be able to get the job done. The horse that cannot be cured of his bad habits is doomed to a life of misery, unless he becomes so bad that he is useless or dangerous, and in that case may be doomed to destruction. If only he had been trained properly from the outset, he could have led a long and contented life.

Obviously, the aspiring trainer who is too gentle must learn to be aggressive so that he can act with authority, and the person who is too aggressive must cultivate sensitivity. This would seem to involve a personality change, which would, of course, be extremely difficult, especially for adults. However, it does not necessarily involve a personality change. Some adults are habitually gentle in manner and some habitually aggressive, and they behave accordingly when they start training horses because they do not know intellectually when they should go easy and when they should be firm. If they have sufficient intelligence and determination, they can study and *learn* how to act and react effectively in their handling of horses.

It must be said, however, that it is hardly worth the effort for adults who are irrationally *timid* to try to learn to train horses, unless they can arrange to be carefully supervised by an understanding expert over a period of years. And it is practically a crime for adults who are confirmed bullies to try to learn to train horses, whether they have supervision or not.

To children who are timid or overly aggressive, work with horses under the right kind of supervision can be very beneficial. It is a fallacy to think that a horse in itself will teach a child to be patient, understanding, persevering, self-confident, decisive, and responsible. But a good teacher can use the horse as a means of promoting all these characteristics in a child.

Training in the Old Days

The suggestion that it takes intelligence as well as determination for adults to learn to train their own horses often raises questions about the situation in the old days, when horses were a common means of transportation. In those days, did people have to be unusually intelligent in order to learn to train their own horses? No, but in those days people who had to depend on horses usually grew up with them, and learned to understand and handle them as naturally as they learned to speak their native language. (Of course, some were better at it than others.) Now, however, adults who have had little or no association with horses want to learn in a relatively short time what their predecessors picked up through long experience. It does take intelligence to do that.

There is another important thing to consider about the training of horses in the old days. Then saddle horses were ridden regularly and were habituated to working for a living. They covered a lot of miles and saw a lot of sights. Now, most young horses are expected to "get broke" in concentrated schooling sessions. They are given an hour or so of riding, sometimes daily, but more often only two or three times a week. They, too, are expected to learn in a relatively short time what their predecessors picked up through long experience. As horses have no real incentive to learn to work, whether they can absorb intensive schooling without turning sour depends primarily on the skill and understanding of their trainers.

In the hands of a capable trainer, a young horse *can* learn a lot of things in a relatively short time. The capable trainer knows how to communicate new ideas to his horse quickly during his workouts, without subjecting him to undue or prolonged periods of confusion. He knows that unresolved confusion leads to frustration, and frustration leads to resentment.

Poor trainers, who do not know how to establish communication with their horses, invariably sour them when they try to teach them too much too soon. To compensate for their lack of knowledge, they force their horses into a scramble of senseless and fatiguing "busy work" every time they are saddled. At worst, their horses openly revolt and develop dangerous habits. At best, they become sullen, flat-eared tail-switchers.

Although a capable trainer can cram a horse's schooling without souring him, he will be the last to claim that he can *habituate* the horse to performing its new skills in a short time. He will not claim, after only a few weeks' work, or even a few months, that the horse is "made" or "foolproof." He will say only that the horse is "green but well started." Horses, like people, are awkward and unsure at new endeavors until they have practiced them for quite some time.

Definition of a Green Horse

Perhaps it would be well here to discuss the term "green horse." It is used widely and often imprecisely. Exactly what does it mean?

To some horsemen, the term green horse covers a multitude of sins. They say it means a horse has been ridden but cannot be trusted to be safe. The horse may misbehave once in a while, or even frequently; however, this is "only because he is green" and not because he has "bad habits." This is the way many trainers of hunters and jumpers use the term. Unfortunately for naïve buyers, some of the bad-acting young horses that the *poorer* trainers of hunters and jumpers excuse as "green" actually are well on their way to being spoiled, and the primary reason for it is that they have been rushed into the exciting work of jumping before they have been thoroughly and capably schooled on the flat.

To Western trainers, a green horse usually is a horse that has been gentled but doesn't know much. The horse accepts a rider and is unlikely to misbehave. However, he is not considered a "broke horse" because he still is clumsy to handle. If a green horse *is* a bad actor, the Western trainer will not say it is because he is green, but he may term the colt "bullheaded" or "silly" or perhaps "bronchy," depending on how he acts, and novices should take this as fair warning that the horse has problems that will have to be overcome before he is worth anything. Whether the trainer himself put those problems in the horse is not a matter than can be discussed tactfully.

In the sense of accuracy, neither of these two definitions of a green horse is adequate. Green means new and inexperienced. Therefore the term green horse in itself means very little. Green at what? Is the horse green at being ridden? Then it should be called green-*broke*, or, if that sounds offensively colloquial to some ears, perhaps a sophisticated term can be invented. What is meant by the term green jumper? Is the horse green-broke *as well as* green at jumping? Or is he well schooled on the flat and new only at jumping? A distinction should be made. The same thing goes for horses that are green in other specialties. Are they green-broke *as well as* green in their specialties? Quite often they are. The reasons are varied. Some trainers don't know any better than to put young horses into advanced work before teaching them the fundamentals of being good riding horses. Others know better but do not want to take the time to school colts properly, especially if they are professionals trying to make money in sales and trying to please owners-in-a-hurry-for-prizes-in-shows.

Definition of Horse-Breaking

This book is written for people who want to know how to give their horses the sound basic schooling that should precede their introduction to any specialties. It is a book about horse-breaking —the right kind of horse-breaking, in which the trainer uses wits instead of brawn to get the job done. (It has been said that the best riders are not those who can stay on bucking horses, but those who can see to it that horses do not buck.) For the sake of some readers, in whose minds the word "breaking" means breaking of spirit, it should be pointed out that most experts use the term with a different connotation. They are referring simply to breaking horses in to being ridden at a walk, trot, and canter. (People don't think anything of saying they are breaking in on new jobs.) The experts try to avoid violence in horse-breaking. Primitive trainers who think that all young horses have to be "bucked out" run the risk of ruining as many horses as they "conquer."

It seems reasonable to assume that anyone who takes the time to find and read books on the training of young horses is prepared to approach training intelligently. Books on horsemanship are nothing more than written advice, and cannot substitute for experience, but they can be timesaving guides to the right kind of experience.

If possible, a novice trainer, in addition to reading books, should seek the coaching and supervision of a good teacher, who can be on the spot to help with problems as they occur. The student will find that it takes time for him to absorb all the advice in a book, and that sometimes while working with his horse he will encounter problems that bewilder him. The teacher can give him the answers at the moment he needs them. Most good teachers, however, recommend reading books on horsemanship, for in the short time they spend with their students they must deal more with specifics than with generalities. Students can save themselves and their teachers a lot of time by broadening their knowledge through reading.

Value of a Good Teacher

The greatest value of a good teacher is that he can see problems developing long before the student is aware of them. The earlier a problem is recognized, the easier it is to solve. The teacher, for instance, will be concerned when he sees a young horse deliberately

freeze in place for a second before complying with a demand to
go forward. He knows the horse is toying with the idea of balking.
He will alert the student and tell him that the next time this tiny
suggestion of balking occurs, he must drive the horse forward with
convincing authority—which may mean a sound whack on the
rump. He also will caution the student not to hold back on the
reins when he corrects the horse, which is something a novice
might do without realizing it. The decisive and rather unpleasant
correction will convince the young horse quickly that balking was
not a good idea at all. A novice trainer, working alone, usually
does not notice problems until they are far more evident. He may
not become seriously concerned about balkiness, in fact, until he
finds that his horse not only refuses to go forward, but bucks,
kicks up, rears, or runs backward when punished for it. If he waits
that long to seek help, it may be too late for the problem to be totally erased, for the balking will have become a behavior trait
solidly reinforced by repeated successes.

The ability to recognize problems early is one of the reasons an
expert horseman seldom comes to violence in his breaking of
young and unspoiled horses. (The term "expert" is being used in
preference to "professional" here because not all professionals are
experts and not all experts are professionals.) Of course, the expert
is not infallible, and he does get into difficulty once in a while,
but he is not inclined to blame the horses for his troubles. He either knows or tries to figure out what he did wrong, or what he
failed to do, and he looks for a new approach. His search for understanding through perfection continues throughout his lifetime.

Abnormal Horses

Are problems in a horse's behavior *always* due to mistakes in training? Not always. There are horses that seem to be congenitally defective, in that their responses do not fit into the normal range,
but they are not as common as second-rate trainers would have
their customers believe. Experts can recognize these horses rather
quickly—sometimes instantly—and, given any choice at all, they
would just as soon not work with them.

One sign of abnormality in a young horse is an almost electric attitude of suspicion combined with a suggestion of viciousness. Today's domesticated equines are not by nature vicious, although they can put up quite a struggle when they are trapped into battle. A normal horse can be *taught* to be vicious, but that is a different matter. The subject here is the young and unspoiled horse. Horses that seem to have a natural and ineradicable trait of wickedness are called "congenital rogues" or "born outlaws." They can be killers.

Another sign of abnormality in a young horse is highly inconsistent behavior in the course of training. An example would be a colt that has unpredictable spells of being spooky. It is normal for colts to be shy of things they have not seen before, and some are more timid and flighty than others. It is part of the trainer's task to accustom young horses to strange sights and gain their trust. It is *not* normal, however, for a young horse to have a tendency to be occasionally and inexplicably alarmed either for no apparent reason or by *familiar objects he ordinarily accepts calmly*. In extreme cases, these horses are or become subject to senseless seizures of panic. They are sometimes called "hysterical" horses, or "loco." In their own way, they are as dangerous as congenital rogues.

What about intelligence? Are some horses actually "dumb" compared to others? Yes. However, more often than not, trainers have trouble with colts they are breaking not because they are too dumb but because they are too smart. In truth, a horse doesn't have to be very smart to learn to accept a rider on his back and carry him around at a walk, trot, and canter. He would have to be smart to learn certain advanced specialties, but he doesn't have to be a prodigy to learn the basics of being a riding horse. It is interesting and somehow gratifying to note that, although horses that are not very bright learn slowly, they learn surely. They are not likely to "lose" what they know. Horses that master their lessons quickly and easily also are clever at finding ways to get out of the work they have learned to do. Their trainers have to stay awake all the time.

Whether a horse is slow-witted or clever, a novice trainer can learn much from working with him. It is the horse that seems to be "touched in the head" that the novice should not attempt to train. But how can inexperienced horsemen discern signs of abnormality in behavior when they have no point of reference? The range of normal behavior is broad. Some colts, for instance, are more temperamental than others, and require more time and sensitivity in schooling, but they are not necessarily "abnormal." They may be only "hot-blooded," which is characteristic of some breeds, notably the Thoroughbred, and of some families within breeds. They can be volatile, but when a trainer sees to it that their energies are properly channeled, they often turn out to be exceptionally good performers. So how can a novice trainer know, if he has trouble with a colt, whether the trouble is his own fault or whether he is working with a defective animal? Obviously he cannot make the determination himself. If he is suspicious, he should seek expert advice, and not wait long to do it.

Of course, a beginner who does not have the advantage of regular coaching by an expert should go out of his way to seek advice *whenever* he runs into trouble he cannot handle. If he is not certain he can even tell whether he is in "real trouble," he should bear this in mind: *If a trainer is not winning, he is losing.* If a horse either has or is developing a behavior problem, and nothing the trainer does brings about improvement, then the horse's undesirable behavior is steadily being confirmed. Whether the horse seems to grow worse or not (and he usually does), the longer the problem exists the deeper the roots are taking hold.

Recognizing an Expert

When it is suggested that the beginner go out of his way to find an expert, going out of his way may be exactly what he has to do. It is a mistake to consider anyone an expert merely because he has been around horses a year, five years, or even twenty years. A businessman who has owned and ridden a gentle pleasure horse for ten years may still be the type who tries to put bridles on backward and forgets to tighten the saddle girth. Even a professional trainer whose office is decorated with trophies and ribbons may be the kind who ruins more horses than he makes. The novice must be careful whom he asks for advice, or he may find himself in more trouble than when he started.

Among professional horse trainers, these are some of the types that may be encountered:

The Crude Trainer. This trainer is totally lacking in sensitivity, and specializes in "knocking horses around" to teach them their lessons. He rarely rides a horse without getting into a battle for supremacy, and he is quite certain that spectators admire him for his dauntless courage. He likes to talk about "conquering" horses. He assumes no blame at all for his many failures. If someone points out that another trainer nearby rarely finds combat necessary, he will nod wisely and say, "Ah, yes, but then he never has had a horse that turned out to be a real problem."

The Confidence Man. This trainer specializes in working for people who are new to horses and horsemanship. Knowing that they do not and cannot realize how long it takes to train a horse well, and want to spend as little money as possible on training, he promises them quick results and sure success. Other trainers, for instance, will not promise to have a horse completely "broke" within a month. He will. He knows he can't do it, but he also knows that when the time comes he can explain to the owner that he ran into unexpected trouble, and probably convince him that "another month will do it." He may be able to keep this going for several months. The sad fact is that he may not be able to train horses at all! A truly capable horse trainer does not have to be a confidence man. He does not have to promise something for practically nothing.

How can a confidence man be recognized by a novice? By his glib promises, and by his rapid turnover in clients, who invariably are beginner horsemen, and also, interestingly, by the fact that he usually is known to his creditors as a poor risk. He just can't be trusted by anyone.

The Ruthless Trainer. This is the trainer who is consciously willing to inflict cruelty and to sacrifice the well-being of his horses to get the results he wants from them. If he works with saddle horses, he will overload their hooves with weights to get "winning action"; if he works with quarter horses, he will ride them into a physical breakdown before they are three years old to win a high-point championship; and if he works with jumpers, he will dose them with anti-inflammatory medications so they can get around show courses on injured legs, when he knows they may suffer permanent damage. If he is asked why he does it, he will say he doesn't like to do it but he must, to satisfy the demands of his customers. "A guy brings me a horse and he wants it to win," one such trainer said. "I know if I won't do what has to be done, there's always another trainer who will. So I really don't have any choice, if I want to make a living." He does the same things to his own horses, and explains this by saying that he trains horses to sell, and "I'd lose money if I took the time to do everything right."

The Horseman. This trainer somehow seems to make a living trying to to do everything right. It is because he is truly an expert. He doesn't have to bow and scrape to fickle customers who don't know anything and don't want to learn anything—he has a waiting list for stalls. When he accepts a horse for training, he does not promise miracles. His acceptance of the horse is his unspoken pledge that he will do his best. He will use all the skill he has to train the horse, and that will include getting tough once in a while if the horse gets tough, but *it is not in his character to be inhumane.*

It is up to the novice to do his best to find the right person to ask for advice, and when he does find the right person, he need not feel that his questions are intrusive into a world of guarded secrets. Only poor trainers, the crude and the ruthless, have bags full of tricks that they jealously hide. Real horsemen have no secrets, and through the ages they have tried to share their knowledge through teaching and through books. Unfortunately, however, their advice often goes unheard. The average beginner *wants* to believe there are secrets. He hopes to find gimmicks that will solve his problems and do his training for him. When he is told that he will have to think and work and develop skill, and that it will take some time, he is disappointed.

Asking for Advice

It must be said that expert horsemen sometimes are reluctant to give occasional advice to beginners, but it is not because they don't want to give away secrets. It is because they know from experience that most beginners do not profit from it. Again and again, they have known this sort of thing to happen:

A novice says his horse tosses its head fretfully and fights the bit. He asks the expert how to cure the problem. The expert replies that the novice is *causing* the problem by jerking and pulling on the reins in a way that makes no sense to the horse. He urges the novice to learn to use his hands correctly, and outlines a program for self-improvement. The novice nods politely, but it is apparent that he has little interest in a complicated answer. Vaguely, he says he will try to follow the advice. He tries one day. The next day he asks a fellow rider what *he* would do about the problem. His friend suggests that he change bits. He tries one new bit, and then another. Each seems to help, but only temporarily. Then the novice reads in a horse magazine that head-tossing can be caused by bad teeth. He calls for a veterinarian, who does find that the horse's teeth have some sharp edges, and files them smooth. The veterinarian also extracts two "wolf teeth" that have grown in wrong. This is good for the dental health of the horse, but it does not cure the head-tossing. Next, the novice notices that a trainer down the road uses draw reins and it occurs to him that these would enable him to hold the horse's head down. So he tries draw reins. This inhibits the head-tossing, but the horse starts charging against the rider's hands. The novice discards the draw reins, exasperated and bemoaning his predicament to all who will listen. He is grateful when a tobacco-chewing old-timer saunters over one day and tells him how to break the head-tossing habit once and for all. The old-timer tells him to hit the horse on the head every time he tosses it. The novice by now is willing to try anything. Whenever the horse tosses its head, he swats it with the flat of his hand. This not only fails to cure the problem—it makes the horse head-shy. Finally, the novice returns to the expert, and asks him if he would mind repeating what he said earlier.

A novice will have to convince an expert of his sincerity if he hopes to be able to turn to him for occasional help. He can start doing this by making a determined effort to follow the first scrap of practical advice the expert gives him. If the advice does not seem to help, he should return to the expert for clarification and additional recommendations. Then he should try again. A novice who proves his good intentions can win the heart of the crustiest old expert—for who can resist the pleasure of helping a person who helps himself, and who thus makes his adviser look good?

Earlier, it was pointed out that the term "green horse" needed clarification. So, too, does the term "novice trainer." Is the novice a beginning *rider* as well as a beginning trainer? This is not unusual in modern times. It used to be only a joke to suggest that someone who never has ridden a horse should start with a horse that never has been ridden. Now many persons are raising colts with the idea of learning to ride them as they learn to train them. This should *not* be done except under the constant supervision of a competent instructor. A young horse being broken to ride needs all the help he can get, and he won't get any from a beginning rider who is necessarily primarily concerned with his own problems. A beginning rider always tenses when trouble occurs, in fear for his own safety, and this is upsetting to a colt. A person should be able to ride well enough to stay physically relaxed and supple when in trouble. He can get away with being tense mentally if he doesn't let the horse feel it.

Beginning riders do not realize it, but they even detract from the training of schooled horses. That is the reason why horses at rental academies develop many bad habits. At a rental stable I once heard a woman complain that she wanted to trade her mount for another because "this one won't do anything but head for the nearest tree and stand in the shade." She didn't know it, but she was lucky. A horse that went out earlier had bolted back to the barn without its rider.

Getting a Head Start

As part of his own education, then, the aspiring trainer who has little or no experience in riding should take lessons on horses already trained. He should go to the best instructor he can find and hope that the instructor will have a string of good schooled horses. Borrowing a neighbor's horse to ride at random or practicing on rental horses without instruction is not as useful at the outset as taking lessons. An instructor helps a student cultivate desirable habits, and hastens the progress of his learning.

In the better riding schools and clubs, students are either surreptitiously or openly divided into three general groups, which are 1. beginners, or otherwise poor riders, who tend to detract from the training of the horses they ride, 2. intermediate students, who can ride reasonably well-schooled horses without teaching them bad habits, and 3. advanced riders, who can actively promote the schooling of horses from a raw start to somewhere within the range of a finished level. Ideally, a student should progress at least to the intermediate level before starting to train his own horse under saddle. While taking the early riding lessons on other horses, he can be attending to the preliminary "ground schooling" of his own horse—accustoming it to handling, and teaching it good manners.

Self-assurance in riding gives a novice trainer a tremendous advantage in schooling his own horse. It does not guarantee that he will do the job as easily or as well as an expert, but, if he is dedicated to learning, it is unlikely that he will "ruin" his horse, and he may even produce one that is well above average in performance. And his next horse will be better, and the next one better yet.

Case Histories

1. THE OUTLAW

It was on a Friday when the man drove into the boarding stable and asked to see the manager. He was excited and pleased because he had bought a pony for only sixty dollars at an auction, and he asked the manager if he would send a trailer for it and keep it over the weekend. He lived out of town, he said, and would return for the pony on Monday.

The manager sent for the pony, and smiled when he saw it. It wasn't really pretty, but it was spotted, and that, he knew, was what caught the eye of the man who bought it. People always like a lot of color. He told one of his stable boys to take the pony to a tie stall.

The boy led the pony to a stall, and tied it securely. Then, as he turned to walk away, the pony lunged at him. The pony's teeth tore at the boy's back, but fortunately the tie rope restrained him from inflicting more than an angry red welt.

The stable manager immediately ordered all the boys at the stable, including his eleven-year-old grandson, to stay away from the pony. He said he would care for it personally. He was an old-time horseman, and he had seen vicious horses before. When they wait until your back is turned to attack, he said, they're outlaws, and no two ways about it.

The next day the manager went into town on business. He was hardly gone before the stable boys had the pony out for a better look. They weren't scared of an "outlaw." The grandson said he wasn't even scared to ride it. He saddled and bridled the pony, then stepped into the stirrup.

But the girth had not been drawn tight enough, and, as the boy tried to mount, the saddle slipped. The pony jumped sideways, and the boy fell to the ground. The pony dived for him, teeth first. The boy, sprawled on his back, threw up his forearm to protect his face, and it was his arm the pony grabbed. The pony held onto the little arm like a bulldog, despite the thrashing efforts of the screaming boy to free himself. The pony held on until he was beaten off by the other boys, who used pitchforks and brooms as weapons.

The boy's injuries were not as severe as they might have been. He had deep wounds and massive bruises on the forearm, and a broken collarbone.

When the owner of the pony called for it on Monday, he was told of the incident and it was a shock and a disappointment to him. He was concerned about the injured boy, and concerned, too, because his own children would be heartbroken. He knew he couldn't keep the pony, and asked what he should do about it.

"The only right thing to do is have the pony put down," the stable manager said. "It's a killer. Outlaw horses are bad enough, but outlaw ponies are worse, because ponies are always around children."

The owner nodded sadly, and left, taking the pony with him.

"I hope he doesn't decide to put it back through an auction," the stable manager said. "Too many times, people are so concerned about losing money that they talk themselves into believing it is all right to 'let the buyer beware.' That's how come this man got the pony in the first place. You never know how many people are going to get hurt before someone puts a stop to it."

2. THE LOCO HORSE

He was an unusually good-looking horse, big for a three-year-old, but well balanced and athletic. Perhaps that was why his owner was so intent on trying to find an expert who might cure his problem. The owner traveled a long way to see a trainer of good reputation. A lesser animal would not have seemed worth the trouble.

The owner was rightly afraid of the horse, even though he was an able rider. It had a way of bolting out of control at unexpected moments. In talking to the trainer, he described it as a "runaway horse." That was what it was, all right, but there was something more to it.

The trainer accepted the horse with the understanding that there were no guarantees of success. He worked with it for two months. He started the training from the beginning, handling, longeing and line-driving the horse as though it had never been trained before. When he started riding it, he did the initial work in a small pen, so there would be no chance of a runaway. Then he graduated the horse to a large arena.

During all this work, however, a strange pattern in the horse's behavior became evident. The horse responded well to the training, and was alert and willing—about four days out of five. Most of the time the trainer could not have wished for a better pupil. But on certain days, if not on the fifth, then on the sixth or seventh, the horse would go berserk.

The interesting thing was that the horse did not necessarily have the spells of violence when it was being worked or ridden. In one instance, it went out of control while it was being led to its watering trough. The trainer was walking alongside the horse when he felt a sharp jerk on the lead line. He looked at the horse and saw its head thrown high and its eyes wide and blank and glazed, standing as though transfixed. That was all he had time to see, for then the horse bolted, knocking him backward to the ground. The horse ran through a stout board fence, splintering the wood in all directions, and continued on until he crashed through another fence. That seemed to slow him down, and he circled anxiously and then stopped. When the trainer reached him, he found the horse trembling and drenched and steaming with sweat. The eyes looked normal again, in that there was life in them, and the horse seemed to be reassured by the trainer's presence.

When the trainer returned the horse to the owner, he admitted defeat. At the owner's request, he rode the horse, and it was one of the horse's good days, and the owner was delighted to see that it had progressed in its schooling far beyond what it had known before.

"Don't be fooled," the trainer said. "This is a loco horse. He's liable to get himself or a rider killed someday."

As it turned out, however, the owner found a use for the horse in racing. Running events were popular in shows for its particular breed. On brush tracks, it was said that sometimes it took four strong men to get the horse to the starting line, but if they could get him "aimed in the right direction" he outran everything in sight. The horse earned quite a reputation for both speed and endurance. He was never cured of his "loco spells."

3. THE CRUDE TRAINER

In the context of this book, the term "crude trainer" refers to one who thinks primarily in terms of physical force in the handling of horses. Although all beginners in horsemanship are crude, most progress into varying degrees of refinement, depending upon their sensitivity. However, some individuals never develop refinement, because they have virtually no sensitivity in their makeup. Raymond was such a man.

Raymond was, in fact, a confirmed bully, who knew how to act refined in his dealings with people, but saw no need for such pretense in training horses. When his horses misbehaved, he usually "hit 'em in the head" in retaliation. If they acted sluggish, even when fatigue was the reason, he "tore into 'em" with spurs until they were lathered with sweat and gasping for breath. And if they didn't stop or turn quickly enough to suit him, he took pleasure in challenging them with his arsenal of bits.

Raymond always felt justified in the brutalities he committed because, as he pointed out, his horses could avoid them simply by doing whatever he wanted them to do. It never occurred to him that the horses might not understand what he expected of them, or that they might be so overwrought by his tactics that they rebelled in desperation. When he caused injury to his horses, as he frequently did, Raymond said he was "sorry, but they asked for it."

Although Raymond was held in contempt by knowledgeable horsemen, he was oblivious to his reputation. He liked to boast of his battles on horseback. One day he visited a boarding stable for the purpose of borrowing hay, and told the story of his latest problem horse.

The horse was a Thoroughbred right off the track, he said. He had held high hopes that it would be a winner in contests of speed in Western shows. The only problem was that it would run fast but was awkward in turning. Raymond tried a variety of severe bits in his attempts to "get control." None, apparently, was severe enough, for no miracle occurred. So Raymond asked a welder to make one for him. The finished product was a curb bit with a thin mouthpiece and ten-inch shanks.

"The bit proved how stupid a horse can be," Raymond said. "Any animal with an ounce of sense would have paid attention to it. But not this Thoroughbred. Let me show you the bit and you'll see what happened."

He opened the trunk of his car, took out the bit, and displayed it for all to see. It was encrusted with dried blood.

"That fool horse almost lost his tongue," Raymond said. "Anyone want to buy him cheap?"

It wasn't long thereafter that Raymond had to give up horse training. He was arrested and sent to prison, not for abusing horses, but for a burglary at a service station.

4. THE CON MAN

Whether young or old, people new to the ownership of horses have daydreams about the future. Many have visions of riding in horse shows and hearing their names called to step forward to claim silver trophies and blue ribbons. They want to *win* something. Lisa was like that. She daydreamed of winning the ladies' barrel racing championship at one of the biggest shows in the country.

Lisa's new horse was a fretful five-year-old bay gelding of unknown pedigree, the prancing, hard-to-manage kind that is always described as "spirited" in advertisements. Lisa couldn't enjoy it as a pleasure horse, but, because it always seemed to want to run, she was sure it would make a barrel horse.

The trainer she met was an extremely nice-looking man who made a point of being modest about his abilities but did say that he had years of experience with horses—in other parts of the country. Somehow he gave Lisa the impression that he had trained and shown with the best, although he never made it clear just where he did it. The thing that pleased Lisa most was that he was excited about her horse. He said he could see that the horse had tremendous potential.

Lisa turned the horse over to the trainer and, because it was only two months before the big show, went to see about entering. The barrel racing event was supposed to be strictly invitational, but she arranged to be accepted.

Lisa didn't want to bother the trainer, so during the first month she limited herself to once-a-week visits to watch him work her horse. She had mixed feelings about what she saw. The trainer could ride the pattern fairly fast but it was plain that he had to use brute strength to turn the horse. Did she have that much strength? The trainer assured her that the horse would be easier to handle after it learned more.

During the second month Lisa went out more often. She was getting worried. She could see now that the horse worked with an angry look, ears pinned back and tail switching. Occasionally it tried to break away from its running pattern. But the trainer, with an infectious grin, told her that the horse acted "naughty" only because it had "a mind of its own." He said it was going to be a winner if she could ride it.

Lisa practiced riding the horse several times the last two weeks. It scared her, because sometimes the horse didn't want to start the pattern, and sometimes, once started, it was hard to guide into the turns. The trainer encouraged her. "You know the horse can do it," he said. "All you have to do is show him who's boss."

Then it was time for the big show. Lisa's excitement was almost unbearable. She was slated to ride the first afternoon. There would be thousands of spectators. She tried to calm herself by deciding that it didn't matter if she didn't win that afternoon—it would be enough to get around the pattern in reasonably good time. The over-all show average was what counted. She must be careful not to knock down a barrel.

Lisa's horse did not knock down a barrel. He did not make any bad turns. In fact, he didn't make any turns at all, because he refused to run the pattern. He balked behind the starting line, and, when she tried to make him go toward the first barrel, he went backward instead. She kicked him. In response, he whirled and bolted out the gate, defying her efforts to stop him.

Sobbing, Lisa said she was going to try again the next day. She did, bravely, with the same result. She withdrew from the competition.

Lisa felt humiliated. She said the worst thing about the episode was that she was a failure and a disappointment to her trainer, who had worked so hard to see her win. She was wrong. The worst thing about it was that the trainer was quite satisfied with the handsome fee she had paid him to play along with her impossible dream.

5. THE RUTHLESS TRAINER

At a horse show, word went out that all Tennessee walking horses were to be inspected before they entered the arena for competition. Any horses with raw or bleeding sores around the pasterns were subject to disqualification. This was vexing to one trainer in particular, for he had a contender for the championship, and he had counted on "soring" the horse's pasterns with a caustic agent to guarantee animation.

"Rules against soring are ridiculous," he said. "People who make them don't seem to realize that when trainers can't use one technique they use another."

"What are you going to do?" a bystander asked.

"Oh, I'm not going to do anything," he replied, "but you can bet the other trainers will."

That night his horse worked with dynamic action, and won its class. As the trainer rode out of the ring, however, he did not pause in the paddock for the usual congratulations. He hastened back to his stabling area. He didn't know whether anyone would notice what he had done to the horse, but he didn't want to risk it.

The evidence was there, to be sure. The trainer had used a hypodermic needle to inject a blistering agent above the horse's hocks, and during the class the burns had erupted through the skin.

"Soring" horses in various ways, or otherwise "doctoring" them to improve their performance, is a practice not limited to the walking horse world. There are ruthless trainers in all specialties, and the American Horse Shows Association is attempting to regulate against the cruelties they inflict.

In this book, an arbitrary distinction is being made between crude trainers and ruthless trainers. Both types are callous to their horses, but generally it can be said that crude trainers are those who mistreat their horses in ignorance and are blatant about it, while ruthless trainers are more knowing, and more secretive. Crude trainers are poor horsemen. Ruthless trainers may have only mediocre ability, or they may be highly skilled in their work with horses. It is possible, certainly, for an individual to have genius without conscience.

CHAPTER II

The Horse You Want to Train

The premise of this book is that you, the reader, either own or intend to buy an untrained two-year-old or three-year-old horse. Regardless of your plans for any later specialized schooling of the horse, you want it first to receive correct basic training. You want to teach it to be an obedient, well-mannered mount, steady in its paces, and comfortable to ride.

When undertaking the basic training of a young horse, be assured that it doesn't matter whether the horse is Western, Saddlebred, or hunter type. The approach is the same. All three types should learn to work agreeably at their natural gaits before anything else is done with them. They should learn to be "pleasure horses" under saddle. After they are well broken in to riding, they can be put into training for demanding show specialties, if that is desired, and their background of good handling will increase their chances of success a thousandfold.

It is impossible to overemphasize the importance of sound basic training as a preparation for exciting work such as racing events, gaited show horse classes, or show jumping. Basic training in itself is exciting to a young horse, because he is unsure of himself in his new role of carrying a rider. Through it, he learns not only to accept a rider, and to go, turn, and stop in response to signals, but to trust the rider's judgment above his own instincts, and to strive to please. When these fundamentals are established, the horse can readily and confidently give its attention to advanced schooling. In addition, the trainer has gained a large measure of assurance that the horse will not become a nervous wreck if it is taken into a specialty that makes the adrenalin run high. This means that the horse can be used as a pleasure mount as well as a show horse, or returned to such use after its show days are over.

Don't ever be misled by trainers who claim (and believe) that young horses should be encouraged and *conditioned* to be easily excitable if they are to be used in show specialties that require maximum effort. They will tell you that "when a horse gets too broke it gets lazy." They do not realize it, but they are confessing that they do not know how to *school* horses to use themselves dynamically.

How Long Will It Take?

Even though you are willing to give your horse a solid foundation in basic training, it's a sure bet that you are wondering how long it will take. This is such a normal question that many authors of books about training horses try to answer it by constructing time schedules for their readers. However, suggesting a time schedule can be misleading. A novice trainer may think he *must* follow the schedule, and that he is a failure if he falls behind it, or that he is rushing his horse if he gets ahead of it. The important thing is to know and follow the sequence of steps to be taken in training, allowing as much time as necessary for the accomplishment of each step. You will discover that your horse learns some lessons quickly, and some slowly. Trying to hold yourself and the horse to an arbitrary time schedule would be unreasonable.

After I started writing this book, I bought a three-year-old filly that was foaled on a ranch in Colorado. She had been handled very little, and was fearful of contact with human beings. She had been given some experience in standing tied at halter, but that was the extent of her training. I worked with her daily, and within a month she was well behaved about grooming and leading, knew the basics of longeing and line-driving, and was carrying a rider at the walk, trot, and canter. Best of all, she had developed a cheerful attitude about people. However, it cannot be said by any stretch of the imagination that her basic training was complete at the end of a month. She had been introduced to working under saddle, and had developed no problems, but she was very, very green. She was uncertain and unsteady in her paces, and still wary of events and sensations that were strange to her. Her lessons remained to be confirmed by months of routine good handling and riding, and by exposure to a variety of experiences at home and away from home.

In your work with a young horse, you may find it wise to spend the first month entirely on handling, leading, and longeing. You may want to devote the next month to confirming the work on the longe and in line-driving. You may decide not to ride the horse until the third month, or later. The decisions should not be made in advance, but during the course of the training. It is all a matter of judgment, based on the progress the young horse is making.

Your ability to "explain" lessons to your horse will be one of the factors determining your rate of progress, but not by any means the only factor. What kind of pupil do you have? Is it a colt you have raised? If so, has it been petted and babied? Does it come from a breeder's farm or a ranch? If so, has it had any handling at all? Is it healthy? Is it physically well developed for its age? Is it placid-natured, or is it hot-blooded? Has anyone tried to train it, and failed?

In regard to the last question, it should be understood that this book is not directed at the subject of retraining badly spoiled horses. If your horse already has acquired a dangerous habit through mishandling, he needs expert attention. His specific problem must be overcome. Even the expert may not be able to set things right, but he has a far better chance of doing it than an inexperienced trainer. Don't make the mistake of thinking that the bad habit might fade away if you let the horse rest in pasture a few months, or if you simply start over from the beginning in the horse's training, as though nothing ever went wrong. That kind of wishful thinking is a waste of time.

If your horse has habits that are annoying but not dangerous, such as refusing to stand quietly for mounting, then by all means you should attempt to overcome them. Unless they are due to a deep-seated nervousness, a horse will not cling to annoying habits

as tenaciously as to dangerous tricks, because they are not as rewarding. Remember that dangerous habits are those that enable
the horse to render his rider temporarily helpless and vulnerable
to injury. They are weapons he has learned to use, such as deliberate and violent bucking, bolting, rearing, or running backward,
with the ever-present threat of falling.

In general, it is in the early stages of its training that a horse
may develop a dangerous habit. This is because everything is new
and unpredictable to the horse, and it is more susceptible to being
goaded or panicked into a violent act, and thus discover its effec-
tiveness. A horse that does not develop a dangerous habit during
its early training, and becomes thoroughly accustomed to being
handled and ridden, is unlikely ever to "turn bad." Unless, of
course, in later years a crude or deliberately cruel rider drives him
to desperation.

Home-Raised Colts

Young horses that have been raised from foals by novice horsemen often have annoying habits. They may have a tendency to
nip or bite, or to be stubborn and willful. It is not because they
have been mistreated, but because they have been babied and petted into brattish behavior. They can become dangerous.

A wise horseman once gave a 4-H Club youngster a bit of advice that should be engraved in the mind of everyone who owns a
young horse. He had stopped in to visit the boy, who was excited
and happy about his mare's new foal. The boy asked when he
should start training it.

"You'll be training it the first time you put your hands on it,"
the horseman said. "If you want it to grow up to be a good horse,
remember this: *No matter how young a colt is, always treat it like
it is a big horse.*"

The horseman went on to explain to the boy that many people
ruin colts they raise by allowing them to develop habits that seem
cute when they are small but that are intolerable when they are
grown.

"Whenever your colt starts doing something that you think is cute, try to imagine how it would be if he were big. Would you want a big horse to back up to you and push against you to scratch him? Would you want a big horse to learn to lean on you when you picked up one of his feet? Would you want a big horse to chase and play with you, and maybe rear and paw at you? Of course not. You would want him to have good manners, and good manners must be taught from the start."

To persons who have never raised colts, the horseman's advice may seem interesting but not particularly important. Won't a colt grow out of "baby" habits of naughtiness? If not, can't he be broken of them readily enough when the time comes? Those who ask such questions miss the underlying significance of the matter of spoiling a colt. What is important is not so much the specific habits the colt develops as it is the attitude that he acquires. If he is allowed to be rough and playful with people and is not made to mind his manners, then he grows up with the confirmed notion that he can push people around, and long before he reaches his mature weight of a thousand pounds or more he will be quite capable of doing it. He will sullenly and fearlessly defy any attempts to change his outlook. The horse that has grown up without respect for humans is more difficult to train than one that has never been handled.

This is why, among experts, the term "pet horse" is a label of contempt. Experts always find it sickening to hear an owner simper that he (or she) can't bear to discipline a colt because it is so "cute" and "has so much personality." If the owner were wiser and *kind enough to do it* he would teach the colt good manners, and thus ensure that it would have a happier life than it would face otherwise.

Attention to Foals

Because it is so difficult not to spoil little colts, it is best not to handle them when they are nursling foals any more than is absolutely necessary for their care. It is to their advantage to halter-break them and teach them to allow their feet to be picked up, so that they will not be afraid of veterinary attention or hoof-trimming. They also will need light grooming if they are kept up in stalls part of the time. Otherwise, however, they should be left to the attention of their mothers.

Raising an orphaned foal without the aid of a nursing mare and without spoiling it is especially difficult. A veterinarian's advice should be followed on feeding the colt, but with his approval it should learn to eat solid feed (the doctor may suggest oatmeal) as soon as possible. If the foal must be allowed to nurse liquid, it is better to rig a nursing pail than to bottle-feed it by hand. It will learn that the pail is the source of its milk, and will not be so likely to pester people about feeding whenever it is approached. It will be lonely unless it is provided with a companion, which could be a gentle goat. Once the colt has forgotten about nursing, chances are good that it will get along well with a mature gelding. Many geldings seem to like to be foster parents—when one takes up with a colt it is as protective and devoted as a mare.

If it sounds coldhearted to suggest that foals be given a minimum of handling and patting, it should be realized that colts are not born yearning for the human touch. They can learn to like being patted, but they are just as content to start life naturally with their own kind. (Children usually have highly romanticized ideas about horses wanting human companionship, and even about horses having human ambitions. There was, for example, an eleven-year-old girl who cried bitterly because a young mare was found to be unsound for riding and was to be turned out to pasture to be a brood mare for the rest of her life. "I wanted her to be a show horse," the child sobbed. "Now all she can do is raise colts. What kind of a life is that for a horse?")

Handling Weanlings

Colts usually are weaned when they are six to eight months old, although there is no hard rule about it. Some breeders like to wean them earlier, in order to push their growth on grain, but others feel that this is unnecessary and possibly even unhealthy. Some owners allow colts to continue nursing until their mothers wean them, which will occur when the colts are yearlings if the mares have been rebred. Obviously this role of dual support can

be a hardship to mares in their last months of pregnancy. In domesticated life, where they don't need their mothers so much for
protection and education, colts are quite capable of making it on
their own at six months of age.

As weanlings, colts can be given additional training at halter,
depending on what they need. If they are to be shown in conformation classes, they will have to know how to lead well at the
walk and trot and how to stand quietly at attention, and also
should be acquainted with loading and traveling in trailers.

It is understandable that many owners, children and adults,
who are raising their first colts want to start teaching them something beyond halter-work and good manners when they are
weanlings. They may want to try longeing them—teaching them
to obey voice commands to walk, trot, and canter on a circle on a
long line. Or they may want to start ground-driving them, putting
them in a simple little harness and walking behind them and
teaching them to move forward, turn, stop, and back up. By no
stretch of the imagination is this training *necessary* to the
weanling colt. It is, after all, a preparation for riding, and can easily wait until two or three months before the colt is old enough to
ride. If an owner decides to longe and ground-drive a colt that is
under a year old, he must exercise great caution, not only to avoid
souring the little one about work, but to avoid allowing it to injure itself in any struggles that occur. A colt eight or nine months
old may seem to be strong, but its neck, back, and legs can be severely damaged by twisting and pulling.

Training Yearlings

Even with a yearling colt, the value of longeing and ground-driving is questionable, unless it is an unusually stout youngster that
the owner intends to start riding at eighteen to twenty months.
(Most good trainers prefer to wait until colts are at least two or
three years old before riding them, and then are careful not to
put them under physical stress, knowing that they are a long way
from maturity. Thoroughbred and Quarter Horse racing trainers
are an obvious exception; however, their interest in the economics

of racing takes precedence over their concern about the high inci-
dence of crippling injuries young horses incur on the track.)

If you plan to longe or ground-drive your yearling, consider the
fact that there is less risk of harm to the colt in the driving. Novice trainers often fail to realize how little longeing it takes to tire
and strain a horse of any age—working on circles is much more
demanding than working on straight lines. Simple line-driving of
a colt down a road at a walk, which tires the trainer more quickly
than the colt, is harmless enough and does serve to introduce the
colt to new sights and sounds. But driving involving clever footwork on circles and sharp turns should be avoided.

The owners who do best in raising colts usually are those who
have other horses to occupy their time. Like professionals, they let
the little ones enjoy their infancy, and start them to work at an
appropriate time. When they do start regular training of their
colts as two-year-olds or three-year-olds, they have a significant advantage over many persons who buy young horses outright. They
know their colts have not been spoiled or mishandled, and they
have no ready-made problems blocking their way to progress.

Buying a Young Horse

It is possible, although not always easy, to find and buy unspoiled
young horses, and thereby to save the time of waiting for foals to
grow up. The most likely place to find one is at a breeding farm of
good reputation, although there it may cost more than the buyer
wants to pay. The riskiest place to shop for a prospect is at a horse
auction, particularly the weekly or monthly sale-barn type where
most of the crowd consists of horse traders and buyers for
packinghouses. If you cannot or do not want to buy from a
breeder, and are smart enough to stay away from auctions (where
even the experts get fooled), then your best alternative may be to
get acquainted with a reliable horse trader or dealer. To find a reliable dealer, talk to several of the top horsemen in your area,
and ask for their recommendations.

Whenever a buyer looks for a young horse, he should know the
difference between 1. a colt that has been taught good manners, 2.

a colt that is unspoiled but has had very little handling, and 3. a colt that has learned bad habits. These are listed in order of preference. The first category is much to be desired, but the second also is satisfactory, for an unspoiled colt that doesn't know much can learn easily enough. It is the colt with bad habits that is going to be a trial, particularly if it is so bad that its manners are the reason it is on the market.

At a horse dealer's barn one might see examples of all three types of young horses. The dealer does not raise and train his own colts. He buys them from private individuals, from other dealers, and from auctions. If he is a reliable dealer, you can be sure he has used his best judgment in selecting the horses, and has made an honest attempt since buying them to discover whether they have any serious flaws. He won't show you any dangerous or unsound horses if he can help it. He sends his rejects to auctions. However, this is not to say that all the horses in his barn are perfect little jewels. You still have to use your own judgment in deciding what you want.

Let's pay an imaginary visit to a reputable horse dealer, and look at three colts that are "long yearlings," a term that means they are almost two years old. The colts are kept in box stalls, and so we follow the dealer to the stalls to begin our assessment of their manners.

A Well-Mannered Colt

The first colt, on hearing his stall door slide open, turns with interest toward the dealer, its ears perked forward and its eyes alight with gentle curiosity. It stands easily relaxed as the dealer walks to it, and even lowers its head slightly to accept a halter. The dealer snaps a lead strap to the halter and walks confidently out the door. The colt follows readily on a slack line. Thus far, this colt has scored high on manners.

As the dealer starts down the hallway, leading the colt, it moves up to walk alongside him, still keeping the lead line slack, and not crowding. When the dealer halts, the colt halts. It obviously is pleased to be out of its stall, and starts to look around, but a light check on the lead strap reminds it to be still. The dealer snaps crossties to the colt's halter, steps away, and invites us to take a closer look.

We find that we can run our hands over the colt's ears, neck, back, stomach, and legs without distressing it. We can pick up any foot and hold it easily. Even a sudden lift of a hand toward the colt's face does not seem to frighten it. We ask if we can lead the colt outside.

It is no surprise to find that the colt leads easily at both a walk and a trot, with no pushing or pulling. Even though there is grass underfoot, which must be quite a temptation to a colt on dry feed, it does not try to insist on grazing. We ask the dealer if the colt will stand tied, and he suggests we try it and see. There is a tie rail nearby, and so we fasten the lead strap to it with a slip knot, and walk away. The colt never draws the line tight. It does not paw the ground or appear to be restless. It looks around, but it behaves itself.

When the colt is returned to its stall, it enters quietly, and it stands perfectly still as the halter is removed. From what has been observed, it has excellent manners. Certainly, if we are interested in buying it, we will want to see more of it. We will want to observe its movement while free in a pen or paddock, and will have it examined for soundness by a veterinarian, but we know already that the colt has had some good handling.

An Untrained Colt

The second colt acts differently when its stall door is opened. It backs into a far corner, facing the dealer anxiously. Its ears are sharply forward, its eyes wide open. As the dealer approaches with a halter, the colt shrinks back, its tense and trembling muscles suggesting that at any instant it may dart one way or the other. The dealer pauses, speaks reassuringly, then eases up to the colt. Smoothly, gently, he puts on the halter. The colt relaxes somewhat. However, when the dealer starts to lead it to the door, it resists. A few coaxing tugs encourage it to follow.

After the colt steps through the door, it whirls suddenly to face

Clasping a little colt in the arms and letting him discover he cannot struggle free is one way to introduce him to the idea of submitting to restraint. It is instinctive for a colt to be frightened at first by entrapment. When he yields and finds he comes to no harm, he begins to learn he can trust people. This helps prepare him to accept halter training later. Claire DeCamp and three-day-old foal.

No way to play Games that seem cute when a colt is only three days old can lead to serious problems later. Here, Claire DeCamp discovers that if she touches the hips of her colt, he kicks up his heels. The antic may appear to be harmless, but if a colt is allowed to make threatening gestures, he will quickly become a spoiled brat. As he grows older, he will be far more difficult to train than a colt that has never been handled at all.

A lesson in restraint In the first halter-breaking session with a colt, the trainer may not even try to lead the colt. He simply resists any attempts of the colt to pull away, and waits for the colt to discover that when he yields to the lead line the line goes slack. Jim Fisher and Arabian Colt.

Finding that he cannot escape by pulling on the lead line, the colt stops struggling. The trainer waits, ready to resist any further tests, but it is apparent that the colt is losing his fear of being held by a halter and is even thinking of approaching the trainer. The trainer talks to him reassuringly.

Cautiously stretching forward to make friends, the colt seems to bear no resentment about the lesson just learned. Now that he understands he cannot pull away from the trainer, he is ready to step forward when he feels tension on the lead line. The trainer is in no hurry. That lesson can wait until tomorrow.

Handling the legs of a young horse is an important part of his training. The colt should learn to lift his foot at a signal from the trainer, and to stand quietly while the foot is inspected or cleaned. He should never be allowed to lean against the trainer for support. Marshall Cates and Quarter Horse colt.

Sacking is an old method of teaching a skittish young horse not to fear being touched and handled. The trainer starts by allowing the horse to smell and touch the cloth. Larry Goode and Appaloosa colt.

The horse stiffens and draws back as the trainer starts to rub him with the sacking cloth. The trainer gently but persistently strokes the neck until the horse begins to relax.

Swinging the cloth lightly against [the] horse's shoulder causes him to be a[nx]ious again. The trainer does not flinc[h] the horse acts up, but he does try to w[ork] "under the panic level."

Moving alongside the body of the young horse, the trainer again rubs with a massaging action. Occasionally, when the horse is quiet, he pauses to let him rest and realize he means no harm.

Now the trainer swings the cloth under the horse with a gentle slapping motion. As the horse becomes more and more tolerant of the process, the trainer becomes bolder in his actions, but he never hurts the horse.

The hind legs are not forgotten The cloth is worked around and between the hind legs until the horse accepts it without jumping or kicking.

Up and over the hindquarters The trainer starts working his way up the horse's back, rubbing and slapping. He does the entire sacking process on both sides of the horse.

At the end of the lesson the young horse appears to be bored with the whole thing. The trainer can rub, rustle, and swing the cloth in any manner without arousing anxiety. The sacking process with this horse has taken about thirty minutes. The trainer will repeat it tomorrow, to confirm that he has won the horse's confidence, but it will require less than five minutes.

Learning to stand tied This three-year-old filly wears a nylon halter and is tied with a stout rope. Every precaution should be taken to ensure that a young horse cannot break free in his early tying lessons. If he manages to break loose only one time, he is almost sure to become a "halter puller." However, the horse should be tied with a slip knot, as shown here, so the rope can be released if he struggles and falls. Quarter Horse filly owned by the author.

If a horse is a halter puller he can be tied as shown here. A noose is placed around the girth, and the line is passed through the halter ring. When the horse pulls back to test the rope, the noose draws tight around the girth. The horse quickly discovers that a step forward brings relief from the pressure.

the dealer. Again it is reassured with quiet words. As the dealer leads it to the front of the hallway, it follows hesitantly. The dealer does not fasten this colt in the crossties.

There is little need to check to see whether the colt would accept handling over its body and legs. It would be frightened. Plainly, it is new to being in close quarters with people, and has had little halter training. It does not appear to be spoiled—in its fearfulness it wants to escape, not to attack. It is a good sign that it responds almost gratefully to reassurance.

The dealer offers to take the colt outside so we can see it move, and its actions confirm our diagnosis. The colt does not fight the halter, but it dances around nervously, raising its head and whinnying because it cannot see other horses. It feels very much alone in a strange world. When the colt is returned to its stall, it hurries inside as to a welcome haven. We feel that this colt has acted normally for a youngster with practically no training. Gaining its confidence should not be unusually difficult.

A Spoiled Brat

The third colt is still another story. When the stall door is opened, it turns away from the dealer, as though daring him to enter at the risk of being kicked. The dealer bellows a command to it to behave, and gives it a stinging blow with the lead strap he carries. The colt moves aside, and allows him to put on the halter. Its turned-back ears show its displeasure. When the dealer starts to lead the colt out of the stall, it makes a rush for the door, and is halted only by severe jerks on the strap. Temporarily subdued, the colt walks quietly through the door.

Outside the stall, however, the colt again tries to take charge of the situation. Instead of walking beside the dealer down the hallway, it bulls ahead, jostling the dealer sideways. The dealer has to jerk hard to bring it back to hand, and when he does, the colt nips at him angrily. For this, the colt receives a blow on the neck. It throws its head high and tries to pull away. It is belligerent, not frightened. It is significant that the dealer keeps a wary eye on the colt's front legs, and, when we ask whether the colt has ever tried to strike him with a foreleg, he nods glumly. Without further ado, he adjusts a chain around the colt's nose for better control. This colt is an oversized brat, at the very least. It has no respect for people. It is not a normal untrained colt—it is too sure of itself. There is no doubt that it has been spoiled by mishandling.

The dealer's roughness with this colt is justified, for a horse should never, under any circumstances, be permitted to get away with making deliberately threatening gestures toward people. It must be punished instantly and surely, not in anger, but as severely as necessary to make an impression. The dealer's timing with the punishment is good, and it is noteworthy that he is satisfied to deliver only one blow. Perhaps if he keeps the colt a while he will succeed in teaching it better manners.

If we were interested in buying any of the three colts, we would like to know if anyone has ridden them or tried to ride them. We probably will not be able to find out. They are being presented to us as "not broken to ride," but the dealer himself may not know whether they ever have been mounted. We hope not, because, had they been *successfully* started under saddle, that information no doubt would have come with them. Of the three, the second colt is the one least likely to have been ridden. The first one, despite its excellent "ground manners," could be a problem under saddle if someone gave it a bad beginning in riding it. Ground manners do not necessarily carry over into riding manners. The third colt could be a nasty customer under saddle, although, oddly enough, some horses with ugly ground manners behave fairly decently when being ridden. In making a purchase, we would have to take a chance that there has been no previous riding. It is one of the disadvantages of buying instead of raising a colt.

Preferences in Buying

Assuming that all three colts are pleasing to the eye, we would prefer to buy the first or second. The first has a definite head start in training, but the second promises to come along rapidly. The third is going to have to be straightened out, and it won't be pleasant. Its youth is in its favor, but success in its reform depends on several factors. How long has it been allowed to have its own way? Have we seen the worst of its behavior? Are we able and willing to get tough with it? Generally speaking, a novice trainer will have problems enough in learning to work with an unspoiled colt. He doesn't need to buy someone else's troubles.

A person of little experience with horses might look at the same three colts and reach conclusions that are exactly the opposite of our own. It is not unusual for a nonhorseman to think that a well-behaved colt is "lifeless," or even to scorn it as a "spoiled pet," and to interpret bad manners, on the other hand, as healthy and challenging signs of "spirit." He will not know quite what to make of the timid colt that has never been handled. He may be uneasy about its "spookiness" and decide that it is abnormal.

If a novice trainer knows enough to recognize bad manners in a colt, but wants to buy it because it appeals to him otherwise, he should engage an expert to advise him. The expert will be better able to assess the problem. He may think the novice will be able to handle the colt. Or he may suggest buying the colt and turning it over to a professional trainer for a month or longer for correction. Or he may suggest not buying it. There is a saying in the horse business: "Don't be in a hurry to buy. There's always another horse down the road."

Stable Vices

Up to this point, the consideration of manners of young horses has centered on their behavior toward people. There is another aspect of behavior that should be recognized. Some horses have stable habits that are extremely undesirable, which may be *controlled* to some extent but are all but impossible to *cure*. These include habitual stall-kicking, cribbing (chewing on wood and gulping air), continuous restless pacing, and weaving (swaying the head and neck from side to side). None of these habits can be ignored, because they are injurious to the health of horses. Constant stall-kicking damages legs; incessant wood-chewing can wear incisor teeth down to uselessness; wind-sucking causes bloating and can result in internal damage; and continuous restless pacing or weaving is debilitating.

Habits that are dangerous or destructive and do not lend themselves readily to correction usually are called vices. Some vices are deliberate, as when a horse is wicked about biting. The stable vices listed above are not deliberate acts of misbehavior. They begin as outlets for nervous frustration, and become deeply imbedded disorders. They develop primarily in horses that are kept in isolation and close confinement, with insufficient exercise. Anyone raising colts should take great care to prevent their occurrence. At the first sign of the appearance of a stable vice, every effort should be made to learn the cause and eliminate it.

A buyer who is going to look at a horse for sale might as well assume that he will not be told about it if the horse has stable vices, unless the horse is such an outstanding individual that it is worth all the extra attention it requires. (In a moneymaking race horse or breeding stallion, stable vices are mere idiosyncrasies.) No matter how forthright an owner is otherwise, he usually finds it all too easy to rationalize that a prospective buyer might "exaggerate" the importance of a flaw in stable manners. After all, one can learn to get along with the inconvenience.

Here is an example of rationalization in high places: Not long ago, a woman from the Midwest went to the East Coast to see a five-year-old mare that was for sale at an equestrian institute. The director showed her the mare, but it was not from the director but from a stable worker that she learned, in casual conversation, that the mare was a wind-sucker. The stable hand said she was "the worst in the barn." When the woman asked the director about it, he appeared surprised that she attached any importance to the information. He said lightly that "a lot of show hunters" had the same habit. It appeared that he had not entertained the notion that the woman might not want such a horse, which was, in fact, the case. It was fortunate for her that she had known enough to make inquiries.

It is not always possible to obtain information from stable workers, but a prospective buyer can make his own investigation for telltale signs of vices. Chances are, he will be making more than one visit to a stable to see a particular horse. If he arrives a little early for his second visit, he can hardly be denied permission to go to the stall and look at the horse. This will give him an opportunity to observe it quietly. A snug leather collar around the horse's throat will tell him it is a wind-sucker. Sometimes muzzles are used to prevent the vice. If such devices ordinarily are used but have been removed, then the vice will be self-evident, for the horse, if undisturbed, will be cribbing and gulping air. If the horse is a stall-kicker, it may not be kicking at this particular time, but again there may be devices revealing the problem. The horse may have a short length of chain attached to a hind pastern, by which he inflicts his own punishment when he kicks. Or there may be tires suspended against the walls inside the stall, intended both to discourage the vice and to protect the horse from injury. If the horse is a weaver, this will be obvious. Sometimes a weaver sways from side to side so far that it dances from one forefoot to the other in a weirdly rhythmic movement. As a preventive, some owners hang rubber tires from the ceiling at head height at the front of the horse's stall or wherever it does its weaving.

A veterinarian who is a specialist in horses might discover signs of stable vices during an examination for soundness, and he should mention any that could predispose a horse to unsoundness. However, he can hardly be blamed for failure to discern vices that are not physically evidenced.

Phobias in Horses

There is yet another kind of behavior problem that may exist in a horse, which is more aptly called a phobia than a vice. Fortunately, phobias are the exception rather than the rule in horses. A true phobia is all but incurable, and can be dangerous if a person is unaware of it. A horse may have an exaggerated and uncontrollable fear of a particular thing.

One phobia is a fear of going through narrow openings—stall doors or partly opened gates. A horse with this problem probably at one time was caught in a narrow opening, and is terrified of being trapped again. Instead of stepping quietly through the gate, it is likely to be seized by panic and bolt through it. It can injure itself or its handler. Another phobia is a fear of backing out of a trailer. Some horses scramble back in such fright that they invariably crack their heads against the ceilings of their trailers, and sometimes lose their balance and fall. Other phobias include exaggerated fears of crossing bridges, going through water, and moving in traffic with automobiles. Of course, horses are not born with phobias. More often than not, they are the result of unfortunate experiences during their early handling and training.

It should not be assumed that all signs of fears are signs of phobias. Young unschooled horses are normally timid about new experiences. However, phobias can grow out of normal fears if horses have traumatic experiences that seem to justify their anxieties. If, for instance, a young horse is afraid to cross bridges, and a trainer forces him onto a bridge that gives way with his weight, then he may well develop a phobia. Trainers must take great care not to force their horses into situations that bring them harm. It also is worth noting that phobias in horses can be caused by timidity in their *trainers*. An example of such a problem is given in the case history entitled "Tractor Phobia," later in this chapter.

Unless a seller gives fair warning, there is little chance that a buyer will discover a phobia in a horse until after he has taken the horse home and lived with it for a time. However, young horses that have had little handling are unlikely to have phobias. As pointed out earlier, they are rare in any case. And while a phobia is vexing to the owner, because special handling is necessary, it does not always render a horse useless, for the animal may be normal in every other respect.

Training Older Horses

Occasionally a novice horseman asks about buying an older unbroken horse. Is it more difficult to start a four- or five-year-old horse under saddle than a two-year-old? Not if the older horse is unspoiled. In some instances the older horse may be slower to yield to discipline, but its progress will be steadier, because when it learns a lesson it remembers it. The very young colt will have more ups and downs, gladdening the heart of its trainer with rapt attention one day, and perhaps driving him to distraction with foolishness the next day. And there is a distinct advantage in the greater physical maturity of the older horse. It is less likely to be harmed by stress and strain in training.

It is unusual, however, to find a horse of four years or older that has not been handled and ridden. If a horse has been spoiled, and the idea is to retrain it, it should be clear by now that making a new start with the horse does not eliminate the need to overcome existing problems. It is useless to pretend that the horse knows nothing.

No matter how old a horse is, if it is healthy and alert it is capable of learning new things. But it is extremely difficult for it to unlearn old attitudes. That is why a horse that is supposedly "cured" of a bad habit by an expert can so easily relapse under a poor rider. That is why it is so important for a trainer to see to it that young horses get the right start in life.

On a happier note, it is astonishing sometimes to see how *good* attitudes established in a young horse can remain with the horse even through later years of mishandling. A well-trained horse may have the misfortune of falling into the hands of an owner who mistreats him, and may learn to misbehave in self-defense, and yet still return to its old and good ways under an owner who deserves it.

Case Histories

1. THE FRONT-PORCH COLT

It was the realization of a dream when the Smith family moved from the city to a little farm at the edge of the suburbs. All in the family—the father, mother, eleven-year-old daughter, and nine-year-old son—loved horses and had wanted a place where they could keep them. Now they could even raise a colt, and a friend had given them an old mare in foal.

From the day the colt was born it was fondled and patted. It learned to like being rubbed and scratched, and soon followed the children like a big puppy. Its mother was allowed to graze in the yard in front of the house, and everyone was amused when the colt learned to climb the two steps to get on the large porch where the family often sat to enjoy cold drinks. It liked treats. Especially sugar.

As the colt grew a little older, it became a nuisance, nuzzling and nipping visitors as well as members of the family in its insistence on treats, so it was relegated to the pasture. Still, however, the children played with it. It would allow its forefeet to be lifted until it stood almost straight up, and then, with the forefeet propped against a child's shoulders, would walk on its hind legs. The children called it dancing.

It began to be frightening when the colt was a few months old and started charging at people in the pasture. It seemed to be playing, but it reared and pawed, and once it struck a visitor with a sharp little hoof. It was especially bad about biting. When anyone tried to punish it, the colt would only dodge away and charge again. The best thing to do seemed to be to avoid getting near the colt.

After the colt was weaned, the family decided to work with it a little and try to teach it some manners. A friend who claimed to know a lot about horses said he knew of a cure for the habit of biting. The cure he suggested was sticking two or three straight pins through the colt's lips, and leaving them there, until the mouth became so sore it would hurt the colt to bite anyone. The owners thought it sounded cruel, but they had suffered cruel bites, so they let the friend do it. Within a few days the colt's mouth was so swollen and sore that it couldn't eat. It was necessary to call a veterinarian to remove the pins and treat the inflammation that had developed. He had to drug the colt to near insensibility to do the job. After the colt recovered, its behavior was worse than before. It was turned out and left alone, with the hope that it might grow out of its bad habits.

When the colt was nearly two years old, a trainer was hired to come to the farm and break it for riding. His first visit was the only one. He spent about twenty minutes with the colt, then shocked the family by saying there was no hope of making it into a good saddle horse. He said it was vicious, and although the trait might be controlled by an expert, it could not be erased. The family hired another trainer, who was younger and less experienced and "willing to tackle anything." There ensued a series of battles between colt and trainer. The colt was not afraid of anything, and contemptuous of punishment. It usually received the worst of the engagements, but it did not learn defeat. It learned only to be sly —to feign good manners until it had a chance for a surprise attack. The young trainer meant well, but in truth he put the finishing touches on the family's production of a homemade outlaw.

The conclusion of the story is that the colt finally was humanely destroyed. The family was sorrowful about it. It seemed inexplicable that a colt raised with nothing but love and kindness had turned out to be so bad. But of course that was the trouble. It had received love, but it had not been taught what it needed to know to get along in the world.

2. THE CRIBBER

People who saw the muzzle on three-year-old Ranger in his stall sometimes asked if its purpose was to prevent him from biting visitors. It was not. Ranger didn't have a mean bone in his body. He was a cribber. He had been one since he was a yearling colt, and he would be one all his life.

Without the muzzle, Ranger, when in his stall, would press his upper teeth down on any conveniently protruding board, such as the one along his hay crib, then draw back to stretch his neck, and gulp drafts of air with belching sounds. If allowed to continue, his abdomen would bloat to a stage of acute discomfort.

What causes horses to develop this peculiar vice? In most cases, wind-sucking horses have one thing in common in their backgrounds. At some time when they were young, they were kept in close confinement, apart from companionship with other horses, and were given inadequate exercise.

The day he was foaled, Ranger was sold to a family, but it was agreed that the breeder would keep him and raise him. The colt enjoyed a normal upbringing until it was a yearling. Then, because he was a male and the owners had not decided whether to make him a gelding, he was brought in to be kept in a barn. The breeder had pastures only for brood mares and foals. A little stallion awakening to maturity might be kicked and seriously injured if turned out with mares.

From his stall, Ranger could not even see other horses. In idleness, loneliness, and boredom he began to gnaw on the wood in the stall, and this quickly turned into cribbing. Later he was gelded, and could be put with other horses, but there was no cure for his vice.

Gulping air is a strange addiction, but it is not seen solely in horses. It is known to occur in humans. Sometimes people are unaware that they do it, and learn about it only when they go to a doctor with complaints of bloating and indigestion.

There is no certain answer to the often-asked question of why a particular horse takes to cribbing instead of some other stable vice, such as weaving or stall-kicking. Some trainers believe that a colt is predisposed to it if it is weaned quite early, and many say they have seen horses copy it from one another. Whatever it is that suggests the vice to a horse, it is apparent that isolation and inactivity are the precipitating factors.

3. TRACTOR PHOBIA

The teen-age girl, Kathy, was standing at the doorway of the public stable, talking to friends, when she saw a farm tractor coming in from a pasture. For an instant she froze, all conversation forgotten. Then she turned and ran toward her horse, which was tied to a fence.

She startled the horse into pulling back on his tie rope, but it didn't break. Fingers flying, she unfastened the rope, then led him to the stable at a hurried trot.

"I've got to get Pepper inside," she shouted, pulling on the lead rope. "He's deathly afraid of tractors."

Pepper had not even seen the tractor, but he was bewildered and anxious. Inside the hallway of the stable, the girl patted and soothed him. Then came the sound of the approaching tractor, and, sure enough, Pepper stirred fearfully. Only when the tractor engine was shut down did the girl and the horse quieten.

Somewhat embarrassed, the girl explained that the horse had

"always" had a phobia about tractors. She said otherwise he was perfectly normal. He was, in fact, a horse on which she had won many equitation prizes.

Question: How did Pepper get the phobia about tractors?

Pepper was now six years old. Kathy had owned him since he was three. He had been started under saddle when she bought him, but Kathy had trained him herself as an equitation horse. Everyone thought she had done a fine job, especially in view of her limited previous experience with horses.

The only trouble Pepper gave Kathy in his early schooling seemed unintentional. He was a little spooky about new things. It frightened Kathy somewhat, but she tried not to show it. She was relieved to find that the spookiness usually didn't last long. With soothing and patting, he would relax.

One day when she was riding Pepper on the road, she saw a large tractor approaching. Pepper started prancing anxiously. As the noisy tractor came closer, fear gripped Kathy. This, she thought, could terrify Pepper, and she didn't know what might happen. She tightened her grip on the reins, waiting. Pepper stopped, spraddling his forelegs, watching the oncoming tractor. Kathy decided to play it safe. She turned the horse around and cantered away from the tractor.

Back home, the incident remained on Kathy's mind. She knew she should not have given up so easily. She resolved to go to farms where there were tractors, and try to accustom him to them. She made quite a project of it. She would show him a tractor from a distance, and then try to ride or lead him to it to see that it wouldn't hurt him. It didn't work, because Kathy was afraid of what the horse might do in its fear. The horse, sensing her fear, could hardly be expected to perceive any reason for it other than the immediate presence of the tractor. In his struggles to get away, he was too much for Kathy to handle. And so, instead of gaining confidence, he developed a very real and exaggerated fear of tractors. In his later years, any attempts by anyone to force him to stand in place while a tractor approached caused him to panic.

Kathy never realized that her own timidity as a trainer was responsible for the phobia in her horse.

4. AUCTION BARGAINS

Pete is a fine man who probably never has read a horse book in its entirety, but knows more about handling and taking care of horses than most people can ever hope to learn. He is amiable and honest, and makes a good living in the rental and boarding business. He buys horses from sale-barn auctions for his rental string—and the stories he tells about some of his bargain purchases are worth hearing.

One time, for instance, he bought a nice-looking bay mare, a smooth-mouthed nine- or ten-year-old. She was unblemished and appeared to be perfectly sound.

Before Pete puts horses in his rental string, he gives them a try-out period. His trail guides use them daily, reporting anything noteworthy about their manners and level of training. The new mare was tested and it developed that she had beautiful manners and was exceptionally well trained. She had only one problem. Occasionally she stumbled, and whenever she stumbled, she fell down. For some reason, when she lost her balance even slightly, she could not recover it.

By observation and examination, Pete discovered the cause of the problem. The mare had at one time suffered a severe neck injury. The injury had left her incapable of lifting her head higher than her withers. When she was moving normally, all was well, but when she stumbled, she had no "balancer" to contradict the forward lurch. A veterinarian confirmed that nothing could be done to help her.

More recently, Pete bought a chestnut gelding with a different kind of problem. The horse was healthy and sound, and had excellent "ground manners," but had one wild trick that could flabbergast an unsuspecting rider.

When Pete brought the horse home from the auction he had no inkling of its problem. (Later, he reasoned that it had been tranquilized for its appearance in the sale ring.)

"I let the horse settle in and get used to the place for a few days," Pete said. "In fact, we were too busy for a while to try him out. Everything looked good, though. He acted good-natured and gentle, and would follow anyone around in the lot."

A day came when the press of business eased, and Pete asked one of his trail guides: "How would you like to ride a good horse?"

The trail guide said that would be fine, and so Pete told him to saddle the chestnut gelding. The gelding behaved decorously, until the trail guide mounted him and urged him to go forward.

The horse did not hump its back and start bucking, nor did it rear, nor did it try to run away. It simply squatted low on its hindquarters and then took a mighty leap into the air.

"It was just like a move of the Lipizzan horses of Austria," Pete said, "except it was pretty wild. As soon as the horse landed on the ground it crouched down and did it again. By about the third leap I managed to get to him and jerk him off balance enough to give the trail guide time to get off."

The dismayed trail guide gave Pete a long, unsteady look.

"Can I ride something else?" he asked. "I've decided I don't like good horses."

As Pete points out, in this day of easy accessibility to drugs for use on horses, even an experienced horseman is at a disadvantage when buying at auctions. However, Pete takes it in his stride when a horse doesn't work out. It isn't as though he is a novice trying to find a personal dream horse at a bargain price.

5. THE UNSCRUPULOUS TRADER

The term "horse trader" has fallen into disfavor, but it is not necessarily synonymous with "gyp artist." As in any business (the used car business comes to mind), there are dishonest dealers and there are honest dealers. The latter try to the best of their ability to find and sell horses that will suit their customers.

Unscrupulous traders are those who knowingly sell unsound or unsafe horses to unsuspecting individuals. They know how to disguise flaws. With judicious use of anti-inflammatory medications, they can make lame horses go sound. With tranquilizers, they can make dangerous horses appear calm.

Old Sam was typical of the worst of the horse traders. He deliberately bought bad horses if they were attractive, because he could get them for packinghouse prices and sell them for tidy profits. He was not averse to falsifying registration papers to impress prospective buyers. He always dealt with customers who were new to horses. Everyone experienced with horses knew him for what he was.

Sam's one big come-on to customers was the statement: "If you find you don't like him for any reason at all, I'll take him back."

To naïve ears, it sounded as though he meant that he would refund the money paid for the horse. He didn't mean that at all. He meant that he would take the horse back in trade on another horse. And it was *he* who decided whether it would be an even trade, or whether he "needed a little boot." His game was as old as the horse business.

Once in a while, although not often enough, Sam would lose out on a horse deal because a customer caught on to his scheme before it was too late. There was, for instance, the time he sold a heavily tranquilized "Western pleasure horse" to the Lathrop family.

The family bought the horse on a Saturday, took it home, and found out the next day that it bucked, and bucked hard. To be certain that it was the fault of the horse, and not due to poor horsemanship, the father, Bill, immediately called and asked a nearby trainer to check the horse. The trainer rode it despite its best efforts to unseat him, but he pronounced that it was not and never would be a pleasure horse.

On Monday, Bill called the horse trader and asked him to take the animal back, as he had promised.

"The trader said he would show us another horse that we could take in exchange," Bill said. "When I said we didn't want another horse from him, he refused to talk anymore."

Without further delay, Bill called his bank and learned that his check to Sam had not yet cleared his account. So he stopped payment, and then simply waited to see what happened next.

Within a few days the trader appeared at his door. Hat in hand, he was courteous and friendly.

"I'm sorry that horse didn't work out," he said. "He sure fooled me. I thought I would pick him up this morning and take him off your hands. No hard feelings, I hope."

CHAPTER III

Stallions, Mares, and Geldings

There is something about the idea of owning a stallion that appeals to many a novice horseman. It may be because of the many books and movies that romanticize the stallion, depicting him as a wild, free spirit that roams the great outdoors. In fiction, the stallion is lord of his domain, fleet of foot but capable of standing his ground and defeating all natural adversaries. He yields his freedom only to some special person who has an affinity for horses. In some stories, he yields to a man, after a violent struggle in which the man proves his ultimate supremacy. In others, he is won over by a child, usually a young girl, who perhaps finds him injured and cares for him, and so becomes his trusted friend. At heart, he is still a wild spirit, but for this one human being he will do anything.

The very fact that the story line given above is used so often and so successfully in fiction is evidence of its universal appeal. And there is nothing wrong with a good story. However, anyone who is thinking of owning and training a stallion for use as a saddle horse needs to know and consider some real-life information:

1. A stallion is more costly to maintain than a mare or gelding, because he always must have quarters that secure him from association with other horses. He must have a stall, preferably one with access to a solidly constructed, high-walled exercise paddock. At boarding stables that will accept stallions, an extra charge usually is made for their care.

2. Unless a stallion is trained with skill, by an experienced horseman who can see to it that he "minds his manners" even in the presence of mares in heat, he can be dangerous. A sexually aroused stallion can easily become oblivious to his handler or rider. If he is not well trained, any attempts to "get through to him" may be ignored or may incite him to violence.

3. A horse that is allowed to remain a stallion, and yet is not given the opportunity to breed mares to satisfy his natural drives, must be exercised regularly. Play in a paddock is not sufficient. All horses need exercise, but a stallion needs it as an unfailing routine. Otherwise, his pent-up aggression may be released in displays of ill temper.

4. A stallion that is to be used for breeding will not be a "money-maker," no matter how handsome and well bred he is, unless he earns a name in horse shows or on the track and is assiduously promoted through advertising. Even then, he will be competing with many other fine stallions that already are established as proven sires.

5. Only qualified handlers should supervise a stallion in breeding. Otherwise, either the stallion or the mare could be injured. Stallions can be injured severely by mares kicking. In their natural state of free ranges, stallions have bands of mares, and breed the mares when they are receptive. In confinement in civilization, stallions may be presented with mares that are not ready to accept them. To protect the stallions, expert handlers try to judge the right time to breed, and even when they believe there will be no trouble they still hobble the mares. They also control the stallions to prevent them from biting or in any way harming the mares.

It should be apparent that maintaining a stallion is much more involved than keeping a mare or gelding. There is greater cost, greater responsibility, and greater risk. Still, some people want stallions. They either have raised or bought colts and don't want them gelded because they are afraid it might "take away the spirit." Does it? The question deserves to be answered.

When a stallion is castrated, he loses his sexual drive, and with it he loses the associated surplus of aggressiveness. This is not a loss of "spirit" as interpreted by novices—it is interesting to note that the overwhelming majority of champions in the high-stepping Saddlebred show horse classes are mares and geldings, not stallions. A stallion's "surplus" of aggressiveness is not surplus in wild life, where he must fight for his mares. It is surplus in ordinary civilized life, where he not only does not fight for mares but may even be denied them altogether.

It should be said that many expert horsemen do like the extra aggressiveness of stallions. By skillful handling and exacting training, they can control the aggressiveness, so that it surfaces only in the form of boldness. However, it is again interesting to note that very few stallions have been ridden in Olympic jumping and cross-country events. The international stars are geldings and mares.

At what age does the young stallion's aggressiveness appear? Is it necessary to treat him harshly and even cruelly to make him behave? Should women and children train and ride stallions?

When a colt nears the age of one year, he begins to show signs of sexual awareness. As soon as this happens, if the colt is on pasture, a knowing owner will see to it that he is separated from mares, for a teasing colt can be crippled or killed all too easily by a kick from a mare.

Aggressiveness in Stallions

With sexual development, the colt's aggressive tendencies grow. At first, he is not really difficult to handle. He occasionally acts like a little tough guy, but the moods are fleeting. As time goes on, however, he becomes more determined in his moments of rebellion. All young horses have moments of rebellion, but the stallion's attitude is different from that of mares and geldings in that he shows a decided inclination to take the initiative in a struggle. If this aggressiveness is not firmly and consistently controlled, he may become mean or vicious. A mean mare or gelding (not an outlaw) may bite, and bite hard, but when this happens the message is, "You leave me alone and I'll leave you alone." When a mean stallion bites, he attacks with the intent to tear flesh, and he will continue his assault on a retreating victim.

The volatility of young stallions varies according to their individual temperaments, but aggressiveness is a factor to be reckoned with in all of them. Regardless of claims that stallions of certain breeds are "all good-natured" and "easy to handle," they still are stallions. Such claims usually are made by people who personally have trained very few, if any, stallions. They are not made by skilled professionals.

Some years ago, a man who knew how to handle stallions bought a good-natured two-year-old colt. He trained the horse and, in ensuing years, used it extensively for breeding. The stallion had excellent manners. He even was trusted occasionally to let small children ride him in shows, and he did not betray that trust. People pointed to the horse as an example of his breed. "Horses like that are no trouble at all as stallions," they said.

Eventually, the stallion was sold. The new owners were gentle people who did not know how to handle stallions. At first, they pampered the horse, and allowed him to have his way about small things. Soon, as would any other horse, the stallion began to test the authority of his owners. But he showed a stallion's aggressiveness in his testing. It frightened the owners. They tried to make him mind by swatting at him with reins and riding crops. Their constant little attacks only irritated him. The old-timers have a saying for it: "Stallions can't stand being picked at all the time." It wasn't long before the good-natured stallion became an ill-tempered stallion. He was sold again, this time to a man who boasted that he would "knock some sense into him."

The stallion's first contest with his new owner occurred on the first evening at his new home, when the man entered his stall at feeding time. The stallion swung toward the man, threatening to bite. The man was carrying a stout whip, and he used it angrily. He waded into the stallion, with the intent of giving him a merciless beating. The stallion received several blows, but the beating did not last long, because the horse reacted violently and the man quickly realized he had chosen a poor place to do battle. He was in real danger in the confinement of the box stall. He had to retreat. Thus, in their initial encounter, the man tasted fear, and the stallion tasted success. It need hardly be pointed out that the man was inexperienced with stallions.

There were subsequent battles, but the man did not "conquer" the stallion with brutality. He lacked a sense of timing when he inflicted punishment. Because he was fearful and unsure (although he would have denied it), he punished in anger and he usually did it too late and too long. In a way, the man's problem also was a "surplus of aggressiveness," for he made uncontrolled attacks with intent to do harm, and when he succeeded in forcing the stallion into retreat he continued his assault. The stallion learned the futility of surrender.

The stallion became a dangerous animal. Fortunately for him, he was sold back to the man who originally trained him. The man was able to handle him, and even to improve his disposition somewhat over a period of many months. However, the horse never again was dependable.

It was interesting to hear the comments that people made after the stallion returned. Generally, the thinking was that the owners who caused him to "turn mean" must have treated him with deliberate cruelty. "He was such a sweet, good horse when he left," one woman said. "He never was a bit of trouble to his first trainer."

In truth, the stallion was mishandled, but the cruelty was not deliberate. It was inflicted in ignorance and fear. The first trainer had known what he was doing. He saw to it that the stallion, when young, learned good manners, and he required strict adherence to them. Any suggestions of undesirable aggressiveness always were quelled promptly with convincing authority. They were met with the precise degree of force necessary to subdue them, and no more.

A horseman who is an expert with stallions is characteristically able to meet a challenge instantly and settle it swiftly. He does not "pick at a stallion," nor does he brutalize him. He may have to be tough, even severely punishing, depending upon the degree of the challenge offered, but he is quick and sure, and instead of allowing trouble to build further, he clears the air.

The story of this stallion was related because he represented one of the breeds noted for good disposition. And he did have a good disposition in that he was a steady-tempered animal in comparison with many other stallions. The trainer who handled him correctly had found it relatively easy to teach him good manners. However, the owners who mishandled him found him no coward.

Are Stallions for Men Only?

People often ask whether women should handle, train, or ride stallions. The answer is that only people who are capable of doing so should work with them. There are women trainers who have the expertise. However, women (and men) who cannot find it within themselves to "get tough" with a horse when necessary should not imagine it is never necessary. Such individuals should not train stallions. They should own and ride stallions only if they have the continuing assistance of capable trainers.

Children should not be allowed to try to train stallions. It is highly questionable whether they should even be allowed to ride stallions that are already trained. Adults can readily understand the risk of leading or riding any stallion near a mare in heat. Children may think they understand it, but when with friends or at horse shows they may forget to be watchful. A moment of carelessness can be disastrous.

Even an adult can be inattentive and pay dearly for it. A typical incident occurred at a rodeo in Texas, when a young woman was leading a stallion. She walked behind a mare that was standing tied. The stallion nickered softly. Instantly, the mare lashed out with her heels. The woman was struck on the side of her face. She survived the bone-smashing blow, but plastic surgery was necessary to restore her appearance. Teeth that were not lost in the accident had to be removed to make room for dentures.

Before leaving the subject of stallions, there is a bit of information that might be of interest to readers who have visited or who plan to visit stud farms. There is a little game that some professional trainers like to play with visitors. They like to put on a show to demonstrate how their stallions respond to voice commands with absolutely remarkable obedience. The demonstrations never fail to captivate people—unless they happen to know the secret behind the performances.

There are variations in scripts, but a performance may go something like this: The trainer opens the door to a stallion's stall, steps back into the hallway, and orders the stallion to come to him. Without an instant's hesitation the stallion marches to him, and stands before him like an obedient soldier at attention. "Back!" the trainer orders, and the stallion steps back. "Come here!" the trainer says, and the stallion promptly steps forward. All this (and more, depending on the trainer's showmanship) is done without any physical control of the stallion, for although he wears a halter he is not held by a lead line. Visitors marvel that he does not make a dash for freedom. They know their own horses would, and yet this is a breeding stallion.

What the visitors do not know is that the stallion has a compelling reason to obey the trainer's commands. The reason is in the trainer's hand. It is a folded whip, carried nonchalantly and inconspicuously. The visitors do not attach any importance to the whip, for the trainer never raises it as a threat. But the stallion knows it is there, because he has been "whip-broken."

Whip-breaking is an old technique, widely used in the training of stallions and trick horses. It is not necessarily cruel, if it is done by an expert, but it can be the ruin of a horse if it is attempted and bungled by an amateur. The technique will not be described here, because it is of no concern in this book. Suffice it to say that any horse that is whip-broken is afraid to turn away from a handler carrying a whip. The important point is that no one should accept a demonstration of "voice control" as proof that a stallion has a "marvelous disposition." It *may* be that the horse has been whip-broken because he has a *bad* disposition. Even that is not a certainty, for some professional trainers routinely whip-break all their stallions.

Given a choice between a mare and a gelding, which would you rather own for your personal use as a pleasure or show horse? Some people prefer mares and scorn geldings; some say they "wouldn't have a mare on the place," and others have no prejudices at all.

For and Against Mares

People who prefer mares sometimes claim that it is because mares have more mettle than geldings—more spirit and courage. In the author's opinion, this distinction is more imagined than real. I have known timid mares and I have known dauntless geldings. And although boldness in a horse seems to be an inborn trait to some degree, a trainer has a tremendous influence on the attitude a horse develops. A trainer can cultivate boldness, or he can kill it. Certainly, he will not cultivate it if he *expects* a horse to be weakhearted.

A certain advantage in owning a mare is that she does not necessarily become useless if she is crippled. She can become a brood mare. This is a fact worthy of consideration by people who are sentimental about their horses. When a gelding is unsound and cannot be ridden, he is of no value, and a difficult decision must be made. He must be retired to pasture for the rest of his life (which is costly and may be impractical), or he must be humanely destroyed.

People who dislike mares usually claim that they are troublesome because they are erratic and temperamental when they are in heat. Some mares more than others do have a tendency to be irritable in relation to their heat periods, and some owners allow it to become a problem. They are all too understanding and permissive when their mares are cranky. Thus they spoil their mares, and then throw up their hands and say they will never buy mares again. Perhaps it is just as well.

Novice horseman who do best with mares are those who have never heard that mares are supposed to be difficult. They simply try to handle behavior problems as they occur, whether related to heat periods or not. Novices who are least successful with mares are those who are constantly looking for excuses for their problems with horses. It is convenient for them to say of a mare, "She's always like this when she's in heat." They genuinely believe they are blameless.

There was a family that bought an expensive hunter pony mare for a young daughter to ride and show. The pony was of the Thoroughbred type, in both looks and temperament. She was a hot-blooded handful for the young rider, who tried, unsuccessfully, to make her mind by jerking and pulling fiercely on the bit. As the months went on, the pony became more and more difficult. All problems were blamed on the fact that the pony was a mare. Finally, the family decided to do something about it. The mare was taken to a veterinarian for a hysterectomy. The operation was performed, and the mare no longer had heat periods. But to the surprise and dismay of the family, she remained as high-tempered and disobedient as before, too much for the child to handle.

It cannot be said that proficient trainers entirely ignore the effects of heat periods on mares. A mare that has a tendency to be irritable is not permitted to misbehave, but on the other hand she is not rigidly expected to be at her best level of performance. She may, for instance, be a champion hunter, or cutting horse, or saddle horse, but if she has to perform on a day when she is coming into heat she may not be as keen as usual. A good trainer will be aware of this and will know that the mare did not deliberately stage a letdown.

Generally, whether a horse is a mare or a gelding should be only a minor consideration to a person buying the animal for personal use. It is the individual horse that should be evaluated. If the horse has the appearance, the disposition, and the level of training that the prospective buyer wants, and if it is healthy and free of vices, and the price is agreeable, then it is the right horse.

The Proud Gelding

There is, however, one word of caution to be offered in regard to the evaluation of geldings. There are geldings that are called "proud" or "staggy," and they are to be avoided at any cost. They are geldings that behave like stallions, because when they were castrated the surgery was not completely successful. They are overly aggressive, and quick to turn mean. They cannot be put with mares, because they have sexual drive even though they cannot reproduce. Proud geldings are not common, but they do exist, and those that do exist frequently appear on the market, particularly at auctions and in the hands of unscrupulous traders.

Now that the word of caution has been given, it would be nice to add that it is always easy to recognize a proud gelding. It is not.

Given the right set of circumstances, a proud gelding may offer no hint of stallion behavior. Even a veterinarian may not detect the problem in a one-time visit for an examination of soundness.

If a person knows there is such a thing as a proud gelding, however, he can try to be alert for symptoms.

A woman trainer who knew about proud geldings once narrowly missed buying one from a farmer who was a little slow in telling the truth. She was on a trip in the countryside, and heard that the farmer had a big Thoroughbred gelding for sale. Hoping the horse would be suitable as a hunter prospect, she went to see it.

The horse was a fine-looking five-year-old, and the price was right. The woman rode the horse, using the only equipment the farmer had on hand, an old work bridle and stock saddle. She was delighted with the horse's behavior, for he responded well to her signals and moved calmly at all gaits. Then she dismounted and conversationally asked the farmer to tell her something of the horse's background. She fully intended to make the purchase.

The farmer said he had raised the horse and had planned to race it, but heart trouble and medical bills prevented him from doing so. Therefore, he said, he had only used the horse to ride on the farm.

As the farmer talked, the gelding became restless. He began pawing the ground, ceasing occasionally to lift his head and look far into the distance. Then he neighed loudly, as though calling across the fields. The farmer took the reins from the woman and jerked at the bit, telling the horse to behave. Instead of settling down, the horse became more restless. He collected himself and began prancing lightly in place. The farmer tried to continue talking.

Any horse can become restless and paw the ground and prance and whinny, but it seemed to the woman that the gelding's behavior was like that of a stallion. She remember noting that the gelding had been kept in a stall, not in pasture, and that there was a high-fenced paddock by the barn. There were no other horses in sight.

She interrupted the farmer:

"Is this horse proud?"

"Is he what?" the farmer asked.

"Is he proud . . . is he staggy?"

"Why, not that I know of," was the answer.

That answer in itself was enough to make the woman suspicious. It is a horse trader's favorite phrase, and sometimes it is said in all honesty. But a horse trader can plead ignorance of a horse's problems much more credibly than a man who has raised an animal from a colt to a five-year-old.

This must have occurred to the farmer, for he went on to explain that he "hardly ever" took the horse anywhere, and so, if there was anything wrong, which he doubted, he didn't have much opportunity to find out about it.

The woman almost allowed herself to be convinced. The horse was very handsome. The farmer might be stumbling over his words because he was trying to be carefully honest. She might be imagining things.

"Would you be willing to accept a deposit on him and let me take him home for a week's trial?" she asked. "If I find he is unsuitable I will return him and you may keep the deposit."

To this, the farmer agreed so readily that she felt a pang of guilt for doubting him. She said she would return the next day with a trailer for the horse.

The next day she returned. The farmer met her with a downcast look.

"I wish you had left your telephone number," he said. "I would have called to tell you not to come. I thought it over last night and I want to say that the horse is just what you think he is."

The woman's first reaction was surprise, and then, not anger, but relief. She thanked the farmer for his honesty. He also was surprised and relieved—so much so that he volunteered more information.

"Fact is, he's a mean one," he said. "We tried to race him, but he almost killed a jockey who went into his stall at the state fair. After that no one would ride him."

CHAPTER IV

First Handling and
Halter-Breaking

The training of a young horse begins with teaching him to behave well while he is being handled "from the ground." A horse that is gentle and agreeable to being caught, haltered, led, tied, groomed, shod, loaded in and out of trailers, and saddled and bridled is said to have good "ground manners." A horse that is difficult to control either has not been taught manners or has been taught bad manners.

Again it should be emphasized that horses are not born with good or bad manners. Some are disposed by heredity to have a calm temperament, and are more easily trained by novices than are high-strung horses. Quiet horses are less likely to turn minor incidents into crises. However, the fact that a horse is quiet-tempered does not mean that he is stupid—the docile-looking family-type horse can learn to be as nasty a character in his own way as any of his hot-blooded relatives. It is the trainer's job to see that he does not.

The first ground lesson any horse must learn is to submit himself to physical restraint by his trainer. If he is fearful, as he will be if he never has been in close association with people, then he must learn that there is nothing to fear so long as he does nothing to displease his trainer. If he is not fearful, and is overbearing because he has been mishandled and spoiled, then he must be convinced that his trainer is worthy of respect and obedience.

Regardless of his age, a horse that has had little or no handling has absolutely no conception of the idea of pleasing or displeasing his trainer. He is interested in his own welfare, and will do what he thinks best for himself. In the course of his training he will continue to be interested in his own welfare, but he will learn (or should learn) that his own welfare is best served by trying to do whatever the trainer wants him to do.

Anyone who seriously wants to be a trainer must accept the fact that a horse will *not* generously and diligently co-operate in learning his lessons solely out of affection for his master. He must be taught discipline.

A foal that is only a day or two old can be given a simple little lesson in submission that will leave with him a lasting impression of the superior physical power of humans. (The superiority is fictional, but the horse need never know it.) The trainer can kneel by the foal and clasp him in his arms, one arm around the chest and one around the hindquarters, and hold him in place for several minutes. The foal will struggle to free himself, but he should not be allowed to escape. It is instinctive for him to struggle, and so, when he yields and finds he has come to no harm, he will not only have learned of the power of people, but he also will have *his first inkling that people can be trusted above instinct.*

If the trainer has done his part correctly, he will have held the foal as one would hold a frightened bird, not gripping him tightly to keep him from *trying* to escape but *enclosing* him to *prevent* his escape. The idea of showing a horse that when he struggles he is only making things hard on himself is a vital concept of control applicable in all stages of training.

A horse would never be truly useful to people unless he learned to trust them over and above the dictates of instinct. He is by nature a timid animal. In nature, there are herbivorous animals, which feed on plants, and there are carnivorous animals, which hunt and kill to eat. The former are not fighters by nature— horses, like deer, are creatures whose best defense is flight from danger. They are the hunted. When something unseen rustles in a bush, they want to shy and bolt away. They feel threatened. A lion, on the other hand, might crouch and move stealthily toward the rustling bush, in search of prey. (Imagine how strange it would be for a horse to do that!) Horses are fighters only when they have no other choice.

Halter-Training a Foal

A foal that has been given an early lesson or two in restraint in a trainer's arms is easier to halter-break when the time comes. A little halter can be fashioned or purchased for him when he is about two weeks old. It should be well fitted. The first halter lesson is again only one of restraint. There is no need to attempt to lead the colt. Simply attach a lead shank to the halter, and allow the colt to test it. When the colt tries to pull away and feels the strange pressure on his head, he will be frightened, and he will struggle. Stand impassively holding the lead line, letting the colt discover for himself that when he yields to the line he finds immediate relief from the pressure. If you find it difficult to remain impassive, it may help to imagine that you are a hitching post to which the colt is tied. Your hands should be held somewhat higher than the colt's withers, for then the colt cannot brace his forefeet to pull as hard as he might otherwise, and there is less risk that he will injure his neck.

The foal probably will struggle only a few minutes, for his earlier lessons in handling will have given him an element of confidence in his trainer. If everything is true to form, the struggles will be intermittent during the few minutes, and the two hardest tussles will be the first one and the last one. In his first reaction, the colt fights in surprise and fear. Then he makes several lesser attempts at resistance. Finally, when he understands the situation, he deliberately puts forth his best effort in one last test of authority. On losing that round, he gives up. Then he can be set free. His first lesson is complete.

The "one last test" by the pupil in a learning situation is a phenomenon well known to discerning trainers. It occurs at all levels of training, even in subtle matters. To bystanders, it may appear that the last violent struggle is a renewal of rebellion on the part of the horse, a discouraging sign that things are getting worse instead of better. If a trainer wants to impress novices, he will say, casually, "Now there will be no more trouble." And, to the astonishment of the onlookers, it will be true.

On the next day, the foal may be given a lesson in leading. At least a day's wait is wise because it always pays to give a horse time to absorb important new lessons. New experiences always are upsetting, and too many new experiences at once can be overwhelming. Certainly, in the case of a two-week-old foal, there is no hurry to teach him to lead. It is important for him to be taught to submit to being held by a halter, for he may at times need to be handled. Some trainers, however, like to go on with the leading lesson.

Halter-Training the Older Colt

Before discussing the leading lesson, it must be taken into account that you may have an older colt to halter-train—one that is not so easily overpowered physically. The older colt, whether only a few months old or two years old, needs the same initial lesson in which he learns that it is useless to pull and struggle against the restraint of the halter. The colt may be too strong for you to hold in the struggle, so it will be necessary to tie him to a stout post or tree, and allow him to learn the lesson from the fixed object.

These are rules to observe when tying a young horse to a fixed object:

1. Be certain that the halter and lead line are strong enough not to break when the colt struggles. A good quality rope or web halter and a lead rope with a heavy duty fastener are best to use at this stage. If a colt ever manages to break loose before he becomes *habituated* to standing tied, he will not forget it. He is almost sure to become a "halter puller," which means he will have the irksome habit of testing halters for their strength whenever he is tied. This can prove to be expensive in terms of broken equipment for years to come.

2. The object to which the colt is to be tied must be substantial and unbreakable. Chances are, there is no "snubbing post" in the center of your paddock, and it is hardly worth implanting one

for the halter-breaking of one horse. However, the advantage of a single heavy post set upright in the ground is that there is no way a horse can get his legs caught, as he might in a fence. A tree with a bare trunk is as useful as a snubbing post. It is even better if it has a heavy, clean limb at about the right height for tying, as the limb will have a little flexibility when jerked hard, and there is less chance that the horse will bruise its poll. A hitching rail will do for tying, if it is strong. Do not use a fence rail or board, for it could break or pull loose. The horse would be terrified at finding itself attached to a flying, bounding board.

3. Tie the colt with a slip knot, at a level no lower than his withers if possible. Tie the rope short enough to ensure that the colt cannot become entangled in it. If the colt, by lowering his head, would be able to get a forefoot over the rope, then the rope is too long. The slip knot is necessary so that the colt can be freed if he does get into trouble either by becoming entangled or by falling.

4. The rope should be no longer than necessary for its purpose. A long, trailing end is dangerous to both horse and handler. Any time ropes are used with horses, the trainer must be extremely careful to avoid becoming entangled in it. *Under no circumstances should a trainer ever wrap a rope around his hand, wrist or body, or secure a rope to himself in any way, when he plans to use the rope on or near a horse.*

Some trainers like to use a "body rope" around the horse in the first tying lesson as a precaution against injury to a horse's head or neck. In doing this, a noose is slipped around the horse's girth, with the eye of the noose under the horse, and the free end of the rope is run between the forelegs and up through the halter ring. The horse is tied with this rope instead of a halter shank. In this case the tie most definitely should be above the level of the horse's withers, and there should be very little slack in the rope, else the horse will get his feet over it. When the horse pulls back against this rope, the noose tightens around the girth. The noose relaxes when the horse yields. After a horse has learned to stand tied with a body rope, he will more readily accept being tied with a halter shank. Incidentally, sometimes a body rope is the only answer to the problem of tying an older horse that has a habit of halter-pulling.

Putting on the Halter

If your colt is big, strong, and untamed, you may well ask how you are going to put the halter on his head, and how you can induce him to go to the place where he is to be tied. What if the colt is fearful even of being touched?

A trainer who is skilled with a lariat sometimes chooses to turn an untamed young horse into a paddock, where he can capture him easily by roping him. With the noose settled about the colt's neck, the trainer "snubs" the colt to a post with a half-hitch, quickly taking up the slack in the rope whenever the struggling colt lunges toward the post. When the colt is close enough to the post to be tied, he slips the halter on him and secures him by a lead rope to the post.

If you are not skilled in handling a lariat or other long rope in such a manner, attempting it could be dangerous to both you and the colt. It will be better for you to take the time necessary to gentle the colt to the extent that he will allow you to put a halter on his head.

Assuming that you have a two-year-old that is fearful of being handled, keep him in a paddock for a while and let him become accustomed to you. Make no overt gestures at first. Simply take feed and water into the paddock, and stand by nonchalantly as the horse eats. Find many things to do in the paddock, such as raking and cleaning. The horse will begin to realize there is no great threat in your presence. There is no hurry. A day will come when he will eat grain from a pail in your hands, and allow you to stroke his neck. Finally, you will be able to slip a halter on his head. Then you can use the pail of grain to induce him to follow you to the place in the paddock where you plan to have the tying lesson. You can have the lead rope already tied in place. Snap it to the halter, and immediately step out of the way, before the horse realizes he is tied. The struggle will begin the instant the horse encounters tension on the rope.

The Struggle Against Standing Tied

There is no way of predicting how hard a particular horse will test the halter rope the first time he is tied, but you can be sure there will be a test. At least once, and perhaps several times, the colt will pit his entire weight against the rope. It will cause you a few anxious moments, but if you have taken care to see that the horse is properly tied, he is unlikely to hurt himself. Some trainers, for this lesson, prefer a rope halter with sheepskin padding over the crownpiece and noseband. Some do not tie the horse directly to a fixed object, but to a heavy-duty rubber inner tube that is secured to the object. The tire tube has flexibility but will not break. Whatever you decide to do, and however you do it, you must give the colt a tying lesson before you can go further with the halter-training. Whether the colt struggles lightly or violently, allow him to do the testing without interference, unless he slips and falls and cannot regain his feet. In that event, untie the colt, but tie him again as soon as he is standing. It is doubtful that he will fall again. If the horse is permitted to test the halter fully, and does not break away, he will not challenge it again with such force.

It is good for the older colt to stand tied an hour or more after he has surrendered to the halter. If he begins to paw the ground, you should not reward the pawing with a fuss of attention. You can find better things to do. Perhaps you can catch up on a few barn chores.

Shouting at any horse or punishing him for pawing the ground is likely to make it unduly significant to the horse. He can learn that it annoys and distracts his trainer, and do it intentionally for that very purpose. If pawing is ignored in early training, it seldom develops into a bad habit. (If a horse already has the habit, it may be necessary to hobble his forelegs whenever he is required to stand tied for a lengthy period.)

Halters Can Be Dangerous

You will be tempted to leave the halter on the horse after the tying lesson is completed, so that you can catch him more easily the next day. If you decide to do it, inspect the paddock carefully to be sure there are no projections where the halter might become caught. It is one thing for a horse to struggle when safely tied by a halter rope to a post or tree. It is quite another for him to struggle when the halter is caught and his head is pinned fast. In the latter instance, injury is a certainty. Even death can result.

A loosely fitted halter also is dangerous when left on a horse. It is not unusual for a horse to snag a foot in a loose halter, either by stepping into it with a forefoot when grazing, or by reaching forward with a hind foot to scratch his jaw. If the halter is unbreakable, the horse may fight to his death.

When a halter is to be left on a horse while he is unattended in the paddock, it is a good idea to rig it so that it will give way to a strong pull. This can be done simply by tying the halter together with a piece of twine at the location of the fastener, and leaving the fastener uncaught. The fastener can be secured when you catch the horse for a training session. If the twine seems troublesome, you can attach a weak snap to the halter instead. Remember, however, that the weak snap is to be used only when the horse is unattended—during training sessions, you do not want a "breakaway" halter.

The first leading lesson will be a simple one. All that you want the young horse to learn is to step toward you when he feels tension on the halter, and to follow you when you walk, even though he might prefer to go elsewhere.

Leading the Foal

If you have a young colt that is still with his mother, you can first lead him alongside the mare, then halt him and require him to stay beside you while the mare goes on a short distance. There should be another person present to lead the mare according to your instructions, so that the situation is controlled. After any resistance from the foal is overcome, lead him toward the mare. He will follow willingly. Next, your task is to lead the foal a few yards away from the mare. He will argue about this. To help overcome his resistance, loop a soft rope around his hindquarters, just above the hocks, and, by tugging on the hindquarters loop with one hand, encourage the foal to respond to the halter rope in your other hand. In this way you can avoid a pulling bout with the halter. After the foal has followed and has become quiet (he will be reassured when he sees that he is not leaving sight of his mother), have the mare brought to his side and then release him. Do not release the colt unless he is standing quietly, however. If you release him during a struggle, it will appear to the colt that he won his freedom by fighting the halter.

Leading the Older Colt

It might seem that it would be more difficult to teach an older colt such as a two-year-old to lead than a foal, because of his size, but in most cases it is less difficult. The older colt is not distracted by anxiety about being with his mother. He can pay attention to what you are doing. You need only capitalize on the lesson he learned in standing tied to a fixed object.

Bear this in mind: The young horse has learned to yield to the implacable *resistance* of a *fixed* object. He has *not* learned to yield to being *pulled*.

If there is any one concept that deserves more stress than all others in the training of horses, it is the concept of using *resistance* instead of *pulling* to obtain the co-operation of horses. Only a trainer who understands it, consciously or unconsciously, and applies it in his schooling can consistently produce horses that respond lightly and confidently to his hands, whether they are being led or ridden. A trainer or rider who has pulling hands (usually called heavy hands) will produce horses that pull against him while being led, and are either hard-mouthed or afraid of the bit when being ridden.

With a little thought, a trainer can start learning to use the principle of resisting instead of pulling while he is teaching a young horse to lead. If he has the *tendency* to pull on a horse (which all beginners have) or the *habit* of doing so (which many experienced but inexpert riders have), he can start breaking through it right now. Later, he will get further practice in using resistance instead of pulling in teaching his horse to longe and line-drive, and, finally, he can use the technique in riding. Thus he can teach himself to have "good hands."

Some people think that "good hands" are synonymous with "light hands." Light hands are better than heavy hands, but they are not necessarily good hands in the sense of horsemanship. Good hands are hands that are light most of the time but are not afraid to be strong when necessary, and when they are strong, they are strong in the right way. They do not baby a horse.

Now let's say that your lead rope has been snapped to your young horse's halter, and the horse is ready for his first leading lesson. The horse, having learned not to pull back on the rope, is standing quietly. The rope is slack.

To ask the horse to take a step forward, tighten the lead line enough to apply a little pressure, just enough to see that the horse feels it and is uneasy about it. Then, maintain the pressure as it is, and wait for the horse to do something about it. Do not pull. Pretend, if you will, to be a fence post, not pulling, but ready to resist any struggles by the horse, with as much strength as necessary.

The horse will be discomfited, and will want to find relief. He may start to pull back, but he won't test the rope too hard if he has learned his lesson in standing tied. After a moment, he probably will step forward and find relief from the pressure by slackening the lead line. That is exactly what you want him to do. Leave the line slack for at least a minute, so that he will realize he did the right thing. Then tighten the line again to ask for another step. He soon will get the idea of following to keep the line slack. He will follow somewhat awkwardly, pausing occasionally to see what happens. When he pauses and the line draws tight, allow the line to remain tight, and even increase the tension if he appears to grow tolerant of it, but do not think in terms of trying to pull him forward. Let him discover through trial and error that it is easier and more comfortable for him to follow. (Turning him when he starts to hang back is a clever way to keep him moving, for he has to step into the turn to keep his balance.)

Once in a while a horse that is learning to lead will decide simply to "lean back" against pressure, no matter how much it is increased, not trying to struggle free, but not trying to do anything else, either. This wouldn't matter if he actually were tied to a fence post, for he would weary of it eventually. But it does matter to the trainer, for more than one reason. In the first place, he might weary before the horse does. In the second place, the horse has to learn that whenever the trainer applies pressure to him, the pressure is a signal that the trainer is *asking* for something, and he has to learn that when he receives a signal he must try to find the correct response. It is all right if he tries and makes mistakes, for it is only by experimenting that he can discover what the trainer wants of him, but he *must try*. And so, if the horse merely leans back against the lead rope and does nothing, the trainer will have to make it unpleasant for him, by first slackening the lead line and then giving it a swift tug, smooth but sharp, as though to say, "Pay attention!" He may have to repeat it once or twice to find the degree of severity necessary to awaken the horse into reacting. If the horse is startled into pulling back, the trainer sets himself and resists until the horse yields and steps forward. If the horse does not pull back, but obviously is waked up, then the trainer applies pressure to repeat his request for the step forward.

What if the horse *still* does not grasp the idea of stepping forward? Other measures will have to be considered. With a little foal, a loop of rope around the hindquarters is helpful. With an older colt the success of the technique depends more on the individual horse and the trainer's skill. The hindquarters loop will be more difficult to use if the horse is large and is skittish about being handled, or if, at the other extreme, he doesn't mind sitting back against a rope. It may be more effective to use the noose around the horse's girth as described in the discussion of the first tying lesson. (Sometimes the noose is even more effective when slipped back behind the rib cage.)

When using a rope around the girth or hindquarters of the

older colt, the object is not to pull the horse forward forcibly. A little foal actually can be pulled forward, but a trainer who tries to win a tug-of-war with a horse is wasting his effort, and is letting the horse know its own power. As with the halter rope, the idea is to apply an uncomfortable pressure, so that the horse will step forward to find relief.

Instead of using the rope around the girth or hindquarters, it may be enough to have a friend approach the horse from behind, and, from a safe distance, gently shoo the horse along. When a horse's only problem is his failure to understand, sometimes the simplest answers are best.

Leading the Spoiled Horse

A horse that has been spoiled about leading and has learned (from a heavy-handed trainer) to hang back sullenly whenever he feels like it is not as easy to teach as the unspoiled colt. His trouble is not that he does not understand what the trainer wants. He understands, but he has found out that he is stronger than people, and sees no reason to obey. A reason has to be provided.

If you have a spoiled horse, it probably will accomplish nothing to have a friend urge him along from behind. All this horse would learn from the exercise would be to move willingly forward whenever you had the help of another person. The rope around the girth or hindquarters probably will not help, either, as the discomfort it inflicts is not sufficient to be compelling.

This is a good approach to the problem:

Position the horse so that his right side is parallel to a fence or wall. Stand on the left side of the horse, slightly in advance of the horse's left shoulder, facing the same direction as the horse. Hold the lead shank lightly in your right hand and carry a straight training whip such as a polo whip (about three feet long, with no lash) in your left hand. Hold the whip low at your side, pointing to the rear, so the horse cannot see it. Then, with the lead rope, ask the horse to step forward. If the horse does not obey, flick the whip rearward against the horse's hind leg, snapping him just above the hock. Do not look back as you do this, and do not make any wild gestures. This unexpected little attack will surprise the horse into stepping forward, to escape the threat from behind. He cannot swing sideways, because of the barrier on his right. Continue to work the horse alongside a fence or wall for several sessions, on succeeding days, to confirm your authority.

Sometimes a horse that has shown a tendency to hang back will go from one extreme to the other. Once he starts forward he tries to go faster than the trainer wants him to go. He tries to drag the trainer along, and will succeed in doing so if the trainer tries to hold him back with his own less-than-brute strength.

Before considering any methods of correcting a horse for pulling ahead, the trainer should analyze what he himself is doing. There is a possibility that he is *inviting* the pulling battle.

It is interesting to see, now and then, what a difference there can be between two persons taking turns leading the same colt. One person may have a frustrating time of it, wearing himself out trying to hold the animal down to a slow walk. The other person takes the lead shank and the colt saunters peacefully alongside him with no trouble at all. What is the secret of the easy success of the second person? It is the secret of good hands—hands that can check and resist without pulling. The first person leads with a heavy grip and tries to pull backward as hard as the horse pulls forward. The second person refuses to argue with the horse. When the horse starts to hurry on, the second person lets it "bump into his hand" as though it had just come to the end of a rope tied to a post. If the horse does not yield readily to the fixed hand, the next thing it feels is a sudden yank and release of the halter shank, which checks him at least briefly. If he starts to hurry again, he encounters the fixed hand again, and he either yields to it or is smartly checked again. After one, two, or three times he realizes it is best not to hurry on. There is never a pulling battle, because *the horse is never given anything to pull against*.

A spoiled horse that is aggressive and belligerent about trying to drag his trainer forward will have to be treated more severely. It may be advisable to lead him with a rawhide bosal while he is learning his manners. A smart check with a bosal can be more convincing than a check with a simple rope halter. Sometimes with an ill-mannered stallion a trainer uses a leather halter with the kind of lead shank that has about fifteen inches of chain attached to the snap fastener. He threads the chain through the brass fitting on the leading side of the halter, where the cheek strap joins the nosepiece, and either runs the chain under the jaw and fastens it to the corresponding brass fitting on the other side of the halter, or runs the chain completely around the nose of the horse and snaps it to the same fitting where he started. The chain will be drawn tight when pressure is applied to the lead shank, but will loosen when the line goes slack. Sharp corrective tugs downward or backward on the lead line will have a decidedly punitive action. When this method is used, it should be recognized for what it is—a severe means of controlling a horse that is dangerous to handle.

To return to the assumption that you are working with an unspoiled two-year-old, we will say now that he has learned to walk forward and follow you in response to a signal of pressure on the lead line. In this introductory leading lesson, you need pay no attention to the oft-quoted dictum that "one should never look back at a horse he is leading." The untrained and unspoiled colt does not have any preconceived notions about the direction of the trainer's gaze. Later, when he is accustomed to being led, he might interpret a glance backward as hesitation or doubt on the part of the handler, particularly if he is being led somewhere that he doesn't want to go.

Neither should you worry about breaking any rules against walking ahead of a horse you are leading, unless the colt is behaving dangerously. At present, you are interested only in teaching leading in its simplest form. Allow the colt to follow behind you, but be watchful that he does not tread on your heels. Later, you can teach the colt to walk alongside you, so that you can have closer control.

CHAPTER V

Sacking and Gentling

When a young horse has learned the basics of halter control, it is time for him to learn to allow himself to be touched, rubbed, and handled all over his head, neck, body, and legs.

Teaching a little foal to allow himself to be touched and rubbed is easy. The only real problem is that the little fellow may come to like it all too well, and become a nuisance about it, unless the trainer is careful to set up certain rules of behavior. As emphasized in an earlier chapter, the baby colt must be treated like a "big horse." Rather than patting and fondling him too much, the trainer can accustom him to being touched everywhere by grooming him with a soft brush. He should insist that the foal stand quietly while he is groomed, which is not as difficult as it might seem. The colt will quickly come to like the brushing, and all the trainer has to do is show him that he will brush only so long as he is standing perfectly still. It will become apparent to the colt that any fidgeting or playfulness or pushing against the trainer causes the pleasant stroking of the brush to cease.

An older colt, such as the two-year-old it is assumed you are training, also can be gentled to touching and handling by grooming. However, because of his greater size, it may not be safe for you to try to reach over, under, and behind the young horse with a hand brush. To get the job done quickly, surely, and safely, there is no process better than the old method of "sacking." The only requirement is that it must be done correctly.

Sacking will be described carefully here because it involves another vital principle of horsemanship. Anyone who learns how to do it correctly will gain much insight into the psychology of the horse, and as he does so, he can train himself to take advantage of that insight. There are certain ways a trainer must act and react in working with a horse—he must know when to persist and when to desist. The aspiring trainer must *learn* how to act and react, because it involves overcoming some of his own instincts. People who know very little about horses are likely to "press on" boldly when they shouldn't, making their horses frantic, and to "ease off" timidly when they shouldn't, unintentionally rewarding their horses for undesirable behavior.

First, let it be said that sacking is not a way of "humiliating" a horse, regardless of the anthropomorphic fantasies of movie commentators and magazine feature writers. Again and again, self-styled experts declare that sacking is effective (and somehow base) because it shames a horse into meekness. Nonsense. A horse is born with a sense of self-preservation, but not with a sense of shame. His normal fears of being touched by humans are overcome by sacking because he learns in one or two thoroughgoing sessions that he is not hurt by handling. The horse does not submit because he "loses his spirit." He submits because he gains confidence.

In sacking a horse, a trainer rubs and rustles a large piece of cloth around and over and under a skittish horse until the horse relaxes and accepts it without fear. In the old days, the cloth that was used was a burlap sack, which probably explains the name of the technique. However, a terry cloth towel or a light saddle blanket serves as well. A single sacking lesson may require an hour. Whether it takes that long, or even longer, is insignificant compared to the weeks that might be spent otherwise waiting to see if the horse might become gentle to handling of its own accord.

It is safer not to have the horse tied at the outset of his first sacking lesson. A person who is learning the process of sacking may at some point unduly alarm the horse and cause him to thrash about frantically where he is tied. The horse might lunge backward and then, stopped by the rope, lunge forward, endangering the trainer. At the outset, it is much better for the trainer to hold the halter line in one hand and the sack in the other, and work with the horse in the paddock, so that if he manages to break loose he cannot run far.

The sacking *will* make the horse anxious at first, else there would be no reason for doing it. The idea is to worry the horse just enough to make him anxious but not enough to make him panic. Unless the horse is required to accept a little more than he would tolerate voluntarily, he learns nothing. The trainer himself must be calm, deliberate, and reassuring throughout the lesson.

Procedure in Sacking

With the two-year-old that is our subject, this is the way to proceed with the sacking:

Start by holding the lead shank in the left hand and the sack or large towel in the right. If the horse is suspicious even at the sight of the cloth in your hand, allow him to examine it and touch it with his nose. If he snorts and starts backward, do *not* hastily withdraw the cloth. Calmly hold it as it is, and follow the horse as he goes backward, with no attempt to restrain him. Keep the lead line slack, except when it is necessary to use it briefly to prevent him from turning away. Let the horse go backward until the paddock fence stops him, if he cares to go that far. In this way you have avoided a pulling contest, which you would not be strong enough to win.

After the horse has stopped, encourage him to examine the cloth again. If his anxiety appears to be bordering on panic, do not press him too hard. You must stay under his panic level, else you will lose control of the situation. Your role is to be nonchalantly persistent. When the horse relaxes even a little, lower the sack to your side. Wait a few moments, then show it to him again. Let him discover that when he acts wildly, he gains nothing, but when he becomes still, the cloth is withdrawn. This will reassure him, for it will appear to him that he has discovered how *he* can control the situation. He will become perceptibly calmer.

Next, your objective is to touch the cloth to the side of the horse's neck, back near the shoulder, and hold it there. Take a step toward him and lift the cloth with a smooth, easy motion to touch him. Do it casually but not hesitantly. If you are tentative and delicate, it will seem to the horse that you are creeping up on him with some fearful purpose.

If the horse is startled by the touch of the cloth, and makes a quick move to dodge away, it is again important that you do not involuntarily draw back. This takes self-control. Stay under the horse's panic level, not by fully retreating but by easing off slightly when necessary, and persist in your intent to hold the cloth gently but firmly against his neck. Only when the horse accepts the feel of the cloth, and becomes still briefly, should you lower it. Thus he learns there is nothing to fear, after all.

Throughout this process, remember to keep the lead line light at all times except when using it to correct attempts to turn away. A tight hold on the halter excites the horse's instinctive fear of entrapment in a threatening situation.

Once the horse has accepted the touch of the cloth on his neck, the touch can be gradually turned into a rubbing of the neck, and then the shoulder. From the area of the shoulder, move back to the body. Do this on both sides of the horse, until he not only accepts it but loses interest in it. (At any time when things are going well, you can stop to rest your arm, but the sacking lesson is not yet finished.)

After the rubbing, start gently slapping the colt with the cloth, first on the shoulder, then on the body and legs. As the horse begins to accept it, become more carefree with the cloth. Swing the cloth around, let it rustle and flutter, but do not let it sting the horse. *It should never hurt him.*

Next, rub and tousle the horse again with the cloth, and see if you can work up to the area behind the ears and along and under the jaw. The horse may discover that he likes this "scratching." If he doesn't, he should at least be required to accept a little of it.

Finally, tie the horse and then sack him on the hindquarters, where you could not reach while holding the halter rope.

No two horses will react in precisely the same way to sacking. The majority of unbroken colts will follow a predictable pattern, however. Most will at first want to avoid being touched by the sack, and will try to move away. Some may object only mildly to each new phase in the process, and yield rather quickly, others will be more excitable, requiring more time. Occasionally a trainer encounters a horse that is an exception to the usual pattern in that it shows aggressiveness. This characteristic is most likely to be found in young stallions. If the horse shows any inclination to make threatening gestures (such as striking out with a foreleg), then it is unwise to continue sacking it without taking special precautions. There is a risk of injury, and also a risk of allowing the horse to develop a vicious habit before it is gentled. Whipping a frightened horse to punish it for a reflexive gesture would only frighten it more. The precautions can be humane hobbling devices, but they will not be described here, as the novice trainer should seek expert personal assistance in using them for the first time.

A Lesson in Tact

Anyone who understands what he is trying to do does not think of sacking as a process requiring inordinate patience. Sacking is too fascinating, too challenging of sensitivity and tact, to be boring. Discovering just how much pressure can be put on a horse at any given moment, learning to perceive its limits of anxiety, and finding how to work positively within those limits to produce a trusting and confident animal . . . these things make a person a keener horseman. Later, when the horse is being ridden, he will benefit from having a rider who knows exactly when to "push on" and when to "let up." He is not likely to become a flighty horse that is afraid of his own shadow.

When sacking is done without tact, the results can be pathetic. There was, for instance, a man who had ridden horses most of his life but somehow managed to learn nothing about them. He bought a two-year-old Saddlebred filly and decided to try "sacking her out." He didn't know how to do it, but a friend said it was simple. He was told to slap her with a burlap sack and keep doing it until she submitted calmly. He was cautioned not to quit before the job was done. He took the filly into a paddock, backed her into a corner, and began flailing her with the sack. The filly went into a frenzy of fear, but he had her trapped and he kept swinging. She struggled and scrambled and went down to her knees, repeatedly. Only when she was in a state of near collapse did the man quit. She stood trembling and jerking convulsively, gasping for breath and steaming hot. The man, also exhausted, threw the sack down. "I can't see how sacking is supposed to make a horse calm," he said.

A horse that has been sacked *correctly* by a knowing trainer will be ready the next day to accept grooming of his neck and body with little or no anxiety. He probably will not need another sacking lesson. Daily grooming will complete the job of gentling him to touch.

Handling the Legs

Most young horses are very uneasy at first about any handling of their lower legs, and they are especially fearful of any attempts to pick up and hold their feet. It is as though nature has warned them that their legs must be protected and kept free at all times, so that they can be ready to flee danger. It is no small thing for them to learn to trust people with their legs.

To keep everything simple, do not attempt to pick up your colt's feet until he completely accepts grooming of the lower legs with a soft brush. In the brushing of the legs, start high, near the body, and work down with smooth, sure strokes. It is not necessary to go all the way down the legs the first day, or even the second or the third. The horse will accept a little more each day. It *is* necessary to observe the same rule as in sacking; Don't be fidgety and withdraw the brush whenever the horse acts up a little, or he will learn to act up a lot. If the horse jerks a foot off the ground because the brush has gone lower than usual, you may have to start brushing higher, but don't quit. Brush higher until he relaxes and puts the foot down, then work your way down again. When the horse accepts the brushing at the site where you initially aroused his anxiety, quit and start on another leg.

When working on a hind leg, stand close alongside the hip and face rearward. In this position you are least likely to receive a kick. Horseshoers always stand this way. They may get shoved but they don't get kicked. It is ludicrous to see a person facing a horse from what he only imagines to be a safe distance of two or three feet, stretching to reach a hind leg and brush it. He is a perfect target for the horse. Anyone standing in this manner *must* jump back when a horse acts up, and the result is that he gives his horse a most instructive lesson in dueling with his hind legs.

After the horse has learned to stay quietly for complete brushing of his legs, he is ready to learn to allow his feet to be lifted and held. Or, rather, he is ready to learn to lift his feet for you.

Again, there is no hurry to get it all done in one day. Start with a foreleg. Stand by the horse's shoulder, facing rearward, and run a hand down behind the knee to a point midway or lower between the knee and pastern. Then, with thumb and forefinger, squeeze the back tendon. This strange new sensation *may* cause the horse to lift his leg instantly. If he does, cradle the hoof *briefly* in your other hand and then release the foot quietly before it occurs to the horse to snatch it away. Pause a moment, perhaps to stroke the horse on the shoulder in reassurance and praise for his performance. Then do the same thing with the other foreleg. If nothing more is done the first day, the foundation is laid for success. On the second day, repeat the brief lesson with the forelegs, then apply it to the hind legs.

Your objective always is to induce the horse to lift his leg for you. If you pull to try to lift the foot forcibly from the ground, the horse will discover rather quickly that all he has to do to thwart you is lean on the foot. If squeezing a tendon does not cause the horse to lift his foot, experiment to find something that works. Try tapping the fetlock with the handle of a hoofpick, at first gently and then smartly. Sometimes it is enough to lean against the horse to unbalance him and cause him to shift his weight to the opposite side. Or have someone start to lead the horse forward, and catch the foot as it leaves the ground.

The reason it is suggested that you hold the horse's foot only briefly the first time he gives it to you is that it is best, if possible, to avoid a struggle for control by physical power at the very beginning. If the horse does try to pull his foot free before you can set it down, make every effort within the bounds of safety not to release it until he pauses in his struggle. Then set the foot down. If, however, the horse manages to pull his foot free of your grasp, require him to pick it up again immediately, then set it down.

Allot a short period every day for several days to the training of your horse to allow you to handle his feet. Hold the feet longer and higher each day, until you can hold them as long as you please at the normal height for hoof-cleaning.

Incidentally, do not expect to make progress at the same rate on each of the four feet. It will be nice if you do, but it a curious fact that horses sometimes are more anxious about some legs than others. You may, for instance, have little difficulty with the forelegs of your horse, and with one of the hind legs, and then, to your surprise, find that the horse is afraid to surrender the other hind leg. You may be able to discover a reason for it—perhaps there will be a scar from a wire cut that tells of a bad experience. At any rate, allow more time for progress on that leg. Do not try to hold the foot as high as you can hold the others, at the start. Take your time, and you will overcome his fears.

What should you do if, despite your best efforts to win your horses's co-operation, there is an indication that kicking could get to be a problem?

Make some allowances for the fact that it is normal for a nervous young horse to try kicking once or twice during early handling. So long as you feel that the kicking is only an anxiety response, ignore it and continue with your work to gain his confidence. However, if the kicking continues, and you judge it to be deliberate and increasingly threatening, then it must be stopped by punishment.

To correct the horse for kicking, use a short riding crop. Tie the horse at halter, and stand close alongside his hip, facing rearward. If you have noted that the horse has a tendency to "cow-kick" sideways, you can further avoid the kicking zone by positioning yourself alongside his waist. Then invite the horse to kick, by touching his hind leg or doing whatever it is that he finds objectionable. The instant he kicks, strike him sharply with the crop above the hock. If the blow is swift and sure, the horse will be startled either into crouching defensively or into swinging his hindquarters away from you. Take advantage of the moment of surprise to step backward and doubly assure yourself of safety.

The horse will be wide-eyed and breathless at the unexpected result of the kicking. Let him settle a moment, then pat him and reassure him. (You want him to realize that you are not angry with *him*. It is the *kicking* that you will not tolerate.) When the horse is relaxed and calm, repeat the lesson. He may not kick again. If he does, punish him again. In most cases in the training of young horses, two such punishments are all that are necessary. Older, spoiled horses may require several lessons, on consecutive days. Always handle the legs after punishment, to reassure the horse that no discomfort occurs when he behaves well.

It is inevitable that as your horse gains confidence in allowing you to handle his feet he will at some stage try leaning on you. This is not particularly dangerous but it is exasperating if it develops into a habit. When the horse starts to lean on you, do not release the foot instantly but do not give the horse any support. Speak to him sharply, and bump him with your elbow if necessary to make him straighten up. If you are forced to release the foot to keep from supporting weight, require the horse to lift the foot again immediately. It is easier to prevent this habit from developing than to cure it later.

After your horse has learned to allow his feet to be held, start including hoof-cleaning in the routine of daily grooming. Make it a habit of your own always to set a foot down carefully after cleaning it. It is not fair to the horse to surprise him by "dropping" a foot unexpectedly after he has given it to you confidently. Your aim in all your training is to make yourself predictable to your horse, for this gives him a sense of security.

Handling the Head

One other aspect of handling remains to be discussed. Your horse should learn to allow you to touch and rub his ears and head. If he develops confidence about this now, it will be easier to teach him later to stand quietly for clipping and to accept a bridle and bit.

Every young horse is "head-shy" at the beginning of his training. He is wary of any possible threat to his ears, eyes, nostrils, and mouth. The best way to accustom him to your hands around those vital areas is to include, in his daily grooming, a gentle cleaning of the head with a soft brush and a small, soft cloth. Start by brushing the neck behind the jawline, then stroke behind the ears, then move to the side of the jaw. Next, brush his fore-top, and finally work your way down the front of his face. Use the little soft cloth to wipe his nostrils and mouth, but be certain that you do not at any time cover his nostrils. As to his ears, do no more than stroke them with your hands.

Some young horses are extraordinarily fearful about their ears. If yours seems to be especially touchy, don't press for rapid progress. Unless you raised him, and know that he has never been "eared down," you should allow for that possibility. Someone may have twisted his ears at one time in order to get quick control of him for clipping, or hoof-trimming, or medical attention. It may be weeks before you win his confidence about handling his ears, but eventually he will realize that you can be trusted.

The fact that horses always "pin their ears back" when they anticipate trouble shows how instinctively careful they are to protect them from harm. In a way, it is fortunate for us that they do so, for their ears provide telling clues as to their temper.

Once you have overcome your horse's initial timidity about having his head handled, you must see to it that he is never given reason to become head-shy again. Never strike him on the head or nose in punishment, and never permit anyone else to do so, except in rare instances of emergency. Does that surprise you? Perhaps you have seen riders who are professional trainers cuffing the heads of their horses when they are displeased with them. And perhaps you have been told that a whack on the nose is the best cure for a coltish tendency to nip and bite. Let's put it this way: There may be times when a horse needs to be punished, but why should you punish him in a way that will make him head-shy? Striking a horse on the head or nose for punishment is no more necessary than striking a child on the head or nose. There are other places that can be swatted.

Although you may readily agree that it is unnecessary for anyone to cuff his horse on the head while riding, you may question the advice against hitting the nose as a cure for biting. Regardless of anything you have heard, however, *hitting a horse on the nose is not a dependable cure for biting*. It fails more often than it succeeds, and it not only can make a horse head-shy but can teach him to be mean and tricky about biting.

Hitting a horse on the nose probably *would* cure him of biting if you could be one hundred per cent sure of connecting with your target each and every time he tried to bite, at the instant he did so. You would find, however, that it is all but impossible to be consistent with such punishment. A horse usually nips when the handler least expects it, and he can become quite clever about dodging away from a threatening hand.

A thoughtful trainer who wants to cure a horse of biting must do two things. First, he must analyze his handling of the horse to determine whether he is actually promoting the habit. He must correct his own faults if he expects to get results. Second, he must decide upon a means of punishment that he can employ with consistency.

Hand-feeding of tidbits to a horse, particularly a young horse, can cause the development of a habit of nipping and biting. An expert trainer can hand-feed tidbits without spoiling a horse, but a novice may let the practice lead to undue familiarity. More often than not, the novice thinks it is endearing when the young horse begins to nudge at his pockets and nibble at his sleeve in a plea for treats. It is not so endearing when the nudging and nibbling turns into biting.

Once a young horse has taken up biting, the habit can be encouraged by a trainer who stands carelessly within easy biting range much of the time.

Not long ago, I saw a woman leaning casually against a rail where her horse was tied. She was trying to talk to friends, but was repeatedly interrupted by her horse's attempts to nip at her arm. Each time the horse nipped, she raised a threatening hand and spoke sharply to him. Once or twice she followed through with a slap on the jaw. Still the horse pestered her.

Exasperated, the woman turned to me.

"He's driving me crazy," she said. "What would you do to make him stop?"

"I think I'd move away from him, about three feet farther down the rail," I said.

"That won't solve anything. That won't cure him of the habit."

"No, but at least it won't let him get in any practice while you're talking to your friends."

The point is that a trainer must pay attention to what he is doing. If you have a horse that has a tendency to bite, and want to overcome it, you must work out a plan of action and see to it that he is punished (not merely threatened) *every time* he bites. Do not expose yourself to being bitten unless you are prepared to react decisively.

Trainers have different ways of handling the problem, but this is the method I have found successful:

For about a week, or for as long as it takes to break the horse of the habit of biting, make it a practice never to stand where the horse can bite you unless you have a riding crop in your hand. When you do stand within biting range, carrying your crop discreetly at your side, be on constant alert. The instant the horse tries to bite you, strike a single stinging blow *on his shoulder or on his chest*. With a target area so large, your aim should be infallible, and the horse will feel the punishment as certainly as a blow on the head.

It is far better to use a riding crop than a limp quirt or the end of a halter rope, because it is not necessary to make a wide swing to deliver a sharp blow with a crop. Use wrist action more than shoulder action. Raising your arm or swinging it back before striking delays the punishment, and the horse can see it coming. You don't want him to become fearful whenever you raise your arm. As far as he is concerned, the punishment should "come out of nowhere," and it should occur each time he tries to bite.

After the habit of biting is overcome, do not let it reappear. Don't invite it by letting the horse nuzzle you or rub his head against your shoulder. Even when such gestures do not lead to biting, they are a nuisance. If *you* want to scratch and fondle the horse's head, it is perfectly all right, but if you allow him to rub and push against you, a time will come when you will want to break him of it. He will get so he wants to use you for a scratching post whenever he is sweaty. You may not mind it when you are in your chore clothes, but the horse will not be discriminating.

Use of the Voice

Your young horse, in the course of his daily handling, will come to know you as an individual person. He will not develop the same kind of affection for you that a dog does for his owner . . .

you need never worry, for instance, that he will lose his appetite by pining for you when you are away on a trip. But your manner, your touch, and your voice will be familiar to him. If you earn his trust by being fair and firm, consistent and therefore predictable, your presence will be welcome to him. He may greet you with a nicker when he sees you, or when he hears your voice.

Because your voice is recognizable to him, and because it tells him or reminds him of your presence, eventually it will become an aid in soothing him when he is upset. The assumption here is that you either have or will develop the ability to be soft-spoken and reassuring in times of stress. Trainers who try to steady agitated horses by shrieking, "Whoa! Whoa!" or "Stop that!" usually succeed only in contributing to their excitement. Good trainers, knowing that there is nothing *compelling* about voice commands, rarely yell at their horses. Often their quiet voices are enough to steady their horses, but if they are not, they know what they *do* is more important than what they *say*.

CHAPTER VI

Refining Ground Manners

The old rule that you should not try to teach a horse more than one thing at a time can be misunderstood. It does not mean that a horse must learn one thing well before he can go on to another subject. It is logical and desirable to work on several different "subjects" during every training session. The rule to be observed is that you should only concentrate on one thing at a time in your work.

You can even devise a curriculum for your young horse at this stage. The subjects in his course of instruction now can include: 1. Learning to be agreeable about being caught. 2. Learning to stand quietly while tied at halter for long periods. 3. Learning to behave well during clipping or mane-pulling. 4. Learning not to be afraid of spraying and bathing. 5. Learning to lead correctly at halter.

If it occurs to you that most people give very little positive attention to these subjects during their training of young horses, you are right. Most people are not experts. Instead of assuming responsibility for the ground manners of their horses, they blandly attribute any faults to "personality" differences.

"My horse is always hard to catch because he is such an independent rascal."

"I can't leave my horse tied for any length of time. It's his nature to be restless."

"I have a terrible time pulling my horse's mane because he is so touchy and tender-skinned."

"My horse won't let me use a fly-sprayer on him. He is so afraid of it that I'm sure he thinks it sounds like a snake."

"When I bring my horse into the stable he literally drags me to his stall, because he is such a glutton for feed."

Although such comments reflect vexation, they also reveal an attitude of fond forbearance. The speakers feel that they have found acceptable explanations to excuse the faults of their horses. They haven't the faintest notion that the faults are a result of poor training and handling.

When an older horse has any of the above problems in behavior, he is difficult to retrain. He has succeeded in having his own way for a long time. However, every effort should be made to overcome the faults. From the standpoint of safety, if nothing else, it is particularly important to retrain a horse that is overbearing about leading at halter—an owner who cannot get the job done should employ a trainer who can. Introductory information about retraining a horse that has been spoiled about leading was given in Chapter IV. More information will be detailed later in this chapter.

You can take pride in seeing to it that your young horse learns good manners from the start.

Catching a Horse

After you have gentled your two-year-old, it will be a good idea to arrange for him to be turned out in a pasture on a regular schedule, weather permitting. Colts that can exercise themselves freely throughout the day are much easier to handle and train than those that are kept in close confinement and are always bursting with excess energy.

If the pasture is rich, don't set the colt free on it the first day and allow him to gorge himself. Accustom him to it over a period of several days. Turn him out for only an hour or two the first two days, and for three or four hours a day for the next few days. After that, you can leave him out as much as you like.

The first time you go out to catch your colt in pasture you may have to spend a lot of time catching him, and you may not. If you do, take it in good spirits. Don't give up easily. Don't *run* after him. Let him do the running. Pursue him by walking, taking short cuts across the pasture, and he finally will tire of the game. You will have to use good judgment about carrying a pail of feed to tempt him. If there are other horses in the pasture, they may be a help, but they also may be a hindrance. Greedy horses jostling around you because you have a pail in your hands can be dangerous. When you shoo them away, you are sure to frighten your colt away with them.

When your colt does allow himself to be caught, reward him for it. Take **him** into the stable for a light treat of grain (or his regular ration if it is time for it), and give him a pleasant grooming. Don't put him immediately to work.

If your horse is to stay in pasture at all times, make it a practice to catch him and lead him into the stable at least once every day for a ration of grain. This will give him a pleasant association with your appearance in the pasture. Many owners do not do this, because it is more convenient for them to feed their horses by putting grain in an outside box, or by allowing their horses to run into a shed to eat. They catch their horses only when they intend to work them. Their horses learn that submitting to a halter in pasture is like volunteering for duty. If you simply cannot arrange to bring your young horse in daily for his feeding, at least take a little time at odd moments to go out and catch him when you don't intend to work him at all. Just put his halter on him, give him a pat and perhaps a carrot. Then set him free.

Incidentally, when turning your horse out to pasture, take great care not to let him develop the dangerous habit of pulling his head out of the halter as you unfasten it. His intent will be to whirl and bolt away, and he may kick out with his heels. If he tries to pull free of the halter while you are unfastening it, refuse to unfasten it until he becomes quiet. Put the halter rope around his neck, so that you can hold him steady for a moment after removing the halter. Then, while he is standing quietly, slip off the rope and *you* walk away from *him*. In addition to being careful about how *you* turn your horse out to pasture, give detailed instructions to anyone who offers to do it for you. Inexperienced handlers, knowing no better, sometimes even shoo horses away from them as they release them in pasture, because they like to see them run. They can create problems for you very quickly.

Lessons in Standing Tied

Teaching a young horse to stand quietly while tied for long periods of time is easy to do. All you have to do is let him stand tied, preferably in a busy stable yard, for two or three hours every day for about two weeks.

If you keep your horse at a public stable, you can arrange with one of the stable hands to see that the horse is given this training. (Be certain that the stable hand knows how to tie a horse safely.) If you have your own place and take care of your own horse, you can let him stand tied while you do chores. Remember, however, that half an hour at a time isn't long enough. To accomplish your purpose, you must leave the horse tied for at least two hours at a time. He must learn that being tied is not necessarily a brief experience that is a prelude to doing other things. He must become matter-of-fact about standing tied, and he will.

It will be easier for the horse to accept the lessons if there is some kind of activity going on about him, or if there is another horse or two tied nearby. To the horse, loneliness is the most unendurable of all afflictions. So do not go away and leave him to suffer in isolation.

You will never regret the time spent teaching this lesson to your horse. Wherever you go in the future, whether on trail rides or to horse shows, you will be able to count on the fact that your horse will behave himself when you tie him. You will find yourself feeling sorry for people who are not as "lucky" with their horses.

Clipping

A little clipping now and then keeps a horse looking trim and neat, so you will want to teach your colt to accept it without any fuss. You will find that your experience in the technique of sacking will stand you in good stead in this training. As in sacking, be persistent about introducing the use of the clippers, but take care not to press the horse into a state of panic.

Normally, about all you will want to do is trim away any shaggy hairs behind the pasterns and around the coronet bands above the hooves, clip a "bridlepath" at the poll, and clip under the jaw. You may want to do a little barbering of the ears if long hairs protrude, but there is no need to trim the insides of the ears bare. The hair in the ears gives the horse protection against the invasion of flying insects and other foreign bodies.

If you have a Western horse, you may want to "roach" the mane, clipping it off entirely except for the forelock and a few inches at the withers. However, the racing-type short mane is becoming popular with Western riders, and rightly so, for it helps the horse to whisk flies off its neck in the summertime.

Be sure that your clippers are sharp, so they will not cause any pinching or pulling that will hurt the horse, and be sure they are well oiled, which not only keeps noise at a minimum but protects the clippers. Have your oil can handy while you work, for clippers must be lubricated frequently during operation. Whenever they begin to sound noisy, add oil, a drop at a time, until they are working smoothly. It also is helpful to have some coal oil in a small wide-mouthed container, such as a one-pound coffee can. You can keep the clipper blades clean and free of hair by dipping them briefly in the coal oil occasionally while the clippers are operating.

As a safety factor, you should not tie the horse for the introductory lesson. Ask someone to help you by holding the lead line while you work. If your helper is inexperienced with horses, caution him not to hang onto the line with a tight, heavy grip. Explain that you want him to keep the line light except when the horse tries to pull away. Then he can use it for correction as necessary.

Before starting the clippers, let the horse see them and the attached wiring. Don't make a big thing of it. Nonchalantly rub his neck with the side of the clippers, and flip the wire around a little. Then move six to ten feet away from the horse and turn the clippers on. The horse will be startled, but it is doubtful that he will react strongly at such a distance. Let the clippers buzz for a while, until the horse loses interest, then turn them off. Turn them on and off several times.

When turning the clippers on and off at a distance of several feet from the horse no longer elicits any reaction, leave them on, and, carrying them low at your side but in full view, move to a position by the left side of the horse's neck. The horse will become anxious again, but leave the clippers on until he becomes quiet. Stand facing toward the rear of the horse, holding the clippers in your right hand and stroking his neck with your left hand to reassure him. When he becomes quiet, turn the clippers off. Always turn the clippers off only when he is quiet, as this is his reward for becoming quiet. He must not be given the impression that by acting up he can eliminate the "threat" of the clippers. If he appears at any time to be growing panicky, you can move nonchalantly away a foot or two, then move back.

Again, as in sacking, what you are doing is progressing toward your goal in deliberate stages. The horse is startled by each new move you make, and instantly becomes anxious about *what is going to happen next*. Given a little time to absorb the new move, he realizes (correctly) that it has brought him no harm, and he decides (incorrectly) that you are not leading up to anything else. So he quietens.

Your next move will be to stroke the side of his neck with the flat underside of the clippers while the clippers are buzzing. The strokes will be downward, with the lay of the hair, and you will be moving the clippers backward, not forward, as you do not intend to do any actual clipping. You can accomplish this move cleverly by taking advantage of the fact that you have been stroking the horse's neck with your free left hand. When you are ready to do it, turn the clippers on, and start stroking the neck with your left hand as before. Then lower the hand briefly, and bring both hands up together, *with your right hand holding the head of the clippers against the back of your left hand.* Resume stroking the horse's neck with the palm of the left hand, letting the horse feel the vibration of the clippers through your hand. If you do this smoothly, the horse will be reassured almost as soon as he is startled, and within moments you will be able to remove your left hand and stroke the neck with the clippers alone.

Now you are ready for the actual clipping. Instead of proceeding to the head, start with the legs. If you have done well in training the horse to allow his feet to be handled, you will have little difficulty. Start trimming any long hairs from the backs of the pasterns while the hooves are on the ground. Pick up the feet to finish the pasterns, if necessary, and to do the work around the coronet bands. Trim only the unwanted hair—if you do it well, there will be scarcely any signs that you used the clippers. Careless clipper marks are an eyesore to experts.

The horse will be more fearful of the clipping of his head, even though you have been careful not to make him head-shy. Start by stroking the side of the neck again with the clippers. Then, with your free left hand, rub the area of the bridle path before moving in with the clippers. Clip with short forward strokes, toward the horse's ears. If you try to clip in the other direction, the clippers will be buzzing above the horse's head, and the cord will dangle in his face. He's not quite ready for that experience.

After making the "bridle path," clip under the jaw. Some horses accept this quite readily, others are touchy. Place your left hand lightly on the horse's nose to steady him, and at first work underneath in the wide, soft area back near the throat. When you start moving down the jawline, be extremely careful not to jar the clippers against the bony areas. They are sensitive because they are uncushioned.

The ears come last, and trimming them may be too much to ask of your horse in the first lesson. You might save them for the second lesson. When you do work on the ears, stroke them first. Next, hold one ear gently closed with one hand, and rest the clipper head against the back of the hand so that the horse can feel the vibration. Then, with the ear still held closed, trim the edges from tip to base. If the horse jerks his head away, don't try to hang onto his ear. Let it go, but reach for it again without pause and resume trimming. If you want to trim any extra-long hair protruding from the ears, do this also with the ear held closed, working downward from tip to base. In this way, you will leave protective hair inside the ear. The horse may be better behaved about the clipping of one ear than the other, so be prepared to devote extra time to the ear that worries him more.

After two or three successful clipping sessions, some horses lose all fear of clippers. If your horse is extremely anxious, then ask only a little progress day by day. Use the clippers as part of the routine of daily grooming, but use them only briefly, always quitting on a quiet note. Even if this training requires weeks, it is worthwhile.

Should a "twitch" be used to subdue a horse for clipping? Although I am of the opinion that a twitch, when used to pinch a horse's nose, is not painful so much as it is alarming to the animal, I do not recommend it if the objective is to *train* the horse to tolerate clipping. (I am totally opposed to applying a twitch to a horse's ear, because of the possibility of inflicting injury.) So far as I know, no one has ever trained a horse to submit voluntarily to clipping by using a twitch in any way.

Mane-Pulling

It is customary to pull a horse's mane to thin and shorten it to a length of about three inches when the horse is to be used in fast work such as racing or hunting. Of course, you don't have to shorten the mane at all if there is no necessity for it. (The "necessity" may be dictated by the fashions of horse show circuits.)

At any rate, mane-pulling is not a frightening experience to a horse, and it should not be an unpleasant one. The only trouble is that people have a way of making it unpleasant and even painful. They do it clumsily, then become angry and frustrated when their horses object by shaking their heads and fidgeting. Instead of trying to improve their technique they punish the horses, and they usually succeed in giving the poor animals a lifelong aversion to mane-pulling.

Pulling can be done by the hands alone, but it is simpler, quicker, and easier on the hands to use a pulling comb. The pulling comb is made of metal, it is straight-backed, and its teeth are only about half an inch long. Unlike the regular mane comb, it has cutting edges between the teeth. It is an inexpensive item that should be discarded when old and dull.

It is best to start the pulling near the withers and move forward when working with a young horse or with a horse that has been spoiled. The closer you are to the head, the more difficulty you will have if there is any head-shaking. However, your objective will be to work so carefully and painlessly that by the time you reach the forward part of the neck there will be no head-shaking.

The mane will be thinnest near the withers. As you progress forward into the thicker area, you should thin and shorten the underside of the mane before shortening the top layer. In this way, you will be able to see to it that the mane lies flat and even.

It will be easy to do the pulling painlessly if you use the comb correctly and if you take the time necessary to discover and work within the tolerance level of the horse. Some horses are more sensitive than others.

First, remove all tangles from the mane. Then, starting at the withers, take a very small, flat strand of hair and spread it widely and evenly in the teeth of the pulling comb. The comb should be atop the strand, teeth pointing downward, and it should be at the level where you want the cutting to occur. Wrap the loose end of the strand over the top of the comb once, snugly, then secure it with another wrap at the left end of the comb. Finally, in one smooth and easy motion, pull the comb downward, *weighting the right side so that it pulls and cuts from right to left.* If the hair comes away easily and the horse is not disturbed, then you have not taken too much hair. Try a little more hair each time, to explore for the limit of the horse's tolerance. After you have found the limit, stay within it. In later sessions, you may find that the tolerance level of the horse has risen—this is your reward for breaking him in right.

Until you become skillful at mane-pulling, it will seem a long and tedious procedure. The horse also may grow weary of it. Why not plan on doing only half the mane one day, and the remainder the next?

Spraying and Bathing

Fly repellents, coat conditioners, medicines, hoof dressings—so many products are sold in spray containers that it is a great convenience to have a horse trained to accept spraying calmly. The hissing sound is fearsome at first to all horses, but your young horse can learn to accept it as a matter of routine.

How you handle the horse the first time and every time you use a sprayer on him is extremely important. Don't let it take him by complete surprise. Let him see and hear it operate once or twice, or several times if necessary, before aiming it at him. Be relaxed and reassuring.

Some horses are quick to accept spraying. If yours is not, either because he is unusually high-strung or because he has been mishandled in the past, plan to spend some time on the problem every day for as long as necessary to condition him to accept it. Buy an all-purpose spray bottle, fill it with plain water, and spray him a little every day. On the first day, it is enough to spray only his forefeet. On the second day, perhaps you can spray his forefeet and legs. Keep at it until the day comes when you can spray his entire body.

There are some matters about which horses seem to make sudden decisions, and spraying is one of them. A horse may be troublesome about spraying day after day, improving so gradually that his trainer wonders if it is worth the effort, and then, suddenly, the trouble disappears. The horse becomes perfectly nonchalant about spraying.

Bathing your horse with a water hose should not be difficult. If you are reasonably careful, and start with the water at low pressure (without a nozzle), any problems you encounter will be due more to discomfort than to fear. Very few stables are equipped with temperature-controlled hydrants, so the water probably will be cold. It is helpful to let a horse adjust gradually to a cold stream by allowing it to flow first over his legs, then over his shoulders, back and sides, and finally over his neck and hips. Once he is wet all over, the water will begin to feel good to him, and he will not object to the use of greater pressure.

In this context, you might think of how you feel when you go for a swim in cold water. Plunging into the water can be quite a shock. Unless you are a hardy soul, you probably prefer to wade in and then sink down slowly.

Whenever the stream of water is near the horse's head, *be very careful not to allow any water to enter his ears*. He detests the sensation, and has no way of getting the water out except by shaking his head violently. If water pours into an ear even one time while bathing, he will become head-shy about the water hose. It is better to wash and rinse his head, foretop, and poll with a sponge than to risk an accident.

Advanced Halter-Training

In the horse's further training in leading at halter, start being more exacting in what you require of him. Teach him to walk beside you instead of tagging along behind. Your correct position will be alongside his neck, slightly ahead of his left shoulder, with your right hand on the lead shank eight or ten inches below the snap, and your left hand carrying the trailing end of the shank. It is safer to be in this position than ahead of the horse, for you will have better control of him if he is startled.

If it is difficult at first to persuade the horse to step up and walk beside you, use the tactic described earlier as a method of overcoming a tendency of a spoiled horse to hang back. Lead the horse along a fence line and carry a straight three-foot whip in your left hand. When the horse hesitates, reach back with the whip and tap him just above the hocks. The fence will prevent him from swinging away from the whip—he will have to move forward. Don't look back as you use the whip, or you will unconsciously slow your own walk.

Train the horse to trot as well as walk on the lead line, to make turns to the left *and* right, and to halt on a straight track. *Never allow him to crowd against you.* Make it unpleasant for him the instant he tries it, by a sharp jerk on the lead shank, or by a punch in the shoulder with your elbow.

If your horse starts developing a habit of stopping crookedly, it will not be because it is natural for him to do so. It will be because you are forcefully pulling him to a stop. Reassess your handling of the lead line. Remember that it is your intent to teach him to stop voluntarily in response to a checking signal. If you check lightly, and he does not stop, then check again, harder, but with a jerk, not a pull.

A horse that has learned to lead well always "carries a light line." The halter shank remains limp in the trainer's hand, except for the briefest signals to start forward, turn, or halt. A horse that has learned to lead *exceptionally* well scarcely needs any signals from the lead line. He takes his cues automatically from the movements of the trainer. When the trainer starts forward, he starts forward. When the trainer turns, he turns. When the trainer halts, he halts. He is a credit to the horsemanship of his handler.

A horse that has learned to be a "crowder" will have to be taught a healthy respect for your person. He will have to be shown that, whenever he pushes against you, there are immediately unpleasant consequences. A jerk on the halter or a punch with your elbow may not bother him at all, so you must inflict punishment severe enough to be unpleasant. Leading with a bosal helps, for a bosal has more bite than a halter when it is jerked. However, this may not be enough. It may be necessary for you to make a real show of power by striking him hard with a riding crop on the shoulder.

When a horse crowds on the lead line, it is difficult to deliver an effective blow against the shoulder without first moving aside. This costs something in the timing of the punishment, but you can make your point if you move swiftly. Strike the horse with sufficient authority to astonish and dismay him—if there is no reaction at all, then strike him again *instantly* with enough force to get through to him. You will know you have impressed him if he tries to retreat from you, and if, when you resume leading him, he keeps a wary distance, even though only a little while. Two or three of these unpleasant experiences will give him the basis for a new relationship with you.

Not everyone can administer this kind of punishment intelligently and effectively. Hot-tempered persons who decide to strike a horse seem incapable of limiting themselves to a single significant blow. They give their horses senseless beatings. People who are too tenderhearted or are timid never earn the respect of their horses. They annoy and irritate them with ineffectual nagging and meaningless slaps and swats. Whatever your emotions may be, put them aside, and do what is best for your horse. Give him some rules to live by, and he will be happier for it.

Showing at Halter

Horses that are to be exhibited in conformation classes at horse shows must be taught to stand posed for inspection by judges. Most horses are expected to stand squarely, with their legs straight under them. The exceptions are Saddlebred show horses and others in the "high-tailed" category, which are taught to stand slightly stretched.

It is easier to teach a horse to stand stretched than to teach him to stand squarely, because the requirements of the former are more apparent to the horse. In fact, it is so easy to do it that novice trainers often overdo it. They ask their horses to stretch as far as they can, front legs forward and hind legs back, until they look ludicrously like toy rocking-horses. They are not observant, else they would note that the skilled trainers' horses stand with their forelegs perpendicular to the ground, while the hind legs are stretched back.

To teach a horse to stretch into the proper Saddlebred stance, with the forelegs vertical, the skillful trainer works more with the lead line than with the horse's feet. He tries to coax the horse into answering a signal from the halter to *step* forward into a stretched position. In this way, he encourages the horse to transfer weight to the forehand. A trainer who works primarily by tapping and pulling on the horse's forefeet may cause the horse merely to extend the forelegs, with no transfer of weight.

This does not mean that there is a law against tapping the forefeet, or the hind feet, during training. It means simply that this should be secondary to the use of the halter. Sometimes you will find that you need to tap the feet to help the horse learn to make minor adjustments in alignment after he is stretched.

By the time a horse is ready to be shown in conformation classes, he should be fully trained to answer the halter alone. In showmanship classes, where children are judged on their ability to present a horse in hand, any touching or tapping of a horse on the legs or body is considered a fault.

To teach a horse to stand squarely, with his legs straight under him, a trainer also works primarily with the lead line. By tugging lightly on the lead, he asks the horse to step forward into a square stance. He rarely asks the horse to move backward to correct poor alignment, as this is almost certain to result in an ungainly position. The horse's body can become twisted, or a leg may be turned in or out, or the weight may be shifted too far back.

You can use the lead line to interrupt forward motion, or to "say no" with a check when one foot starts to make an incorrect move.

It will be easier for you to teach your horse to stand squarely if you think in terms of training the legs in pairs. Most professionals work with the hind legs first. Spend several days teaching the horse simply to align his hind feet in response to the halter signal. *See to it that he holds them in the desired position until you give him a definite signal to walk forward.* Practice moving around him while he holds the position. Move in front of him and beside him and to the rear. As a signal to him to step out of the position, move to the spot where you normally stand to lead him, and start him forward. Once you have succeeded in teaching him not to move the hind legs out of position until directed to do so, you will find it surprisingly easy to teach him to bring the forefeet into alignment.

If your horse has good conformation, when he is standing squarely his forelegs will appear to be vertical to the ground, whether viewed from the side or from the front. To make certain the forelegs are vertical from the front view, take care to see that the feet are spaced apart correctly. The hind legs are in correct position when the lower legs, from hocks to fetlocks, appear to be vertical to the ground, whether viewed from the side or from the rear.

CHAPTER VII

Longeing
and Line-Driving

On a visit to the panhandle of Texas one summer, I was told that a man had a good young horse for sale. I went to see it. The horse was two years old, not broken to ride, but gentle. It was in a small corral.

"I'd like to see him move around a bit," I told the owner. "Can we bring him outside?"

The owner had no objections. However, the colt did not lead well enough to trot on the lead line. Attempts to shoo him along only made him travel awkwardly. I wanted to see him move freely.

"Would you mind if I put him on a longe line?" I asked. "I think I can have him trotting a large circle in only a few minutes."

At this proposal, the owner balked.

"I'd rather not let you do that, unless you are pretty sure you want to buy him," he said.

I assumed that he was justly concerned about allowing a stranger to work with his horse. However, his next comment revealed that there was an entirely different reason for his reluctance.

"Fact is," he said, "if I keep the colt I'm going to make a rope horse out of him. The last thing in the world I'd want him to learn would be to run around in circles on the end of a rope."

That *could* present a problem in calf-roping, couldn't it?

If you are planning to make a rope horse out of your colt, you will have to use your own judgment about training it to work on the longe. In general, however, longeing is one of the most useful aids that can be employed in the training of a horse. These are some of the reasons for it:

1. Introducing the discipline of work to the young horse. Until now, you have been concerned primarily with teaching your colt to allow itself to be handled. You have not asked the colt to do any work. In longeing, the colt will learn to respond to commands to perform certain maneuvers and to move steadily at the walk, trot, and canter for as long as you require it. This lays a foundation for discipline later when working under saddle.

2. Exercising. On occasions when you do not plan to ride, but feel that the horse needs exercise, you can give the horse carefully controlled workouts on the longe line.

3. Schooling in collection. When the time comes for it, you can school your horse into gradually increasing degrees of collection by working him in a bitting harness on the longe line.

4. Schooling over fences. If your horse is to become a hunter or jumper, you may want to introduce him to jumping by longeing him over obstacles.

An incidental value of teaching a young horse to work on the longe line will be realized when you introduce line-driving to him. You will discover that it is easy to make a transition from longeing to driving. And line-driving (with the trainer walking behind) has its own values in the basic training of the young horse. By teaching the horse to answer signals from behind to go forward, turn, and stop, it helps prepare him for the experience of being ridden.

Longeing Equipment

What equipment should you have for longeing? Ideally, a longeing cavesson, a cotton or nylon web tape, and a whip, all specifically made for the purpose. However, the cavesson is an expensive item. If you do not care to buy one, use a leather or web halter, one that has metal rings where the cheekpieces join the noseband. Then you can snap the longe line to either side of the noseband, instead of under the horse's jaw. An adequate substitute for a longeing tape is a strong cotton rope, about twenty-five feet long, with a snap attached to one end. The rope should not be so large that it weighs down heavily when used at full length. Neither should it be so small that it might inflict deep cuts if tightly entangled in the horse's legs. You *should* buy a longeing whip. Its stock is five to six feet long, and its lash is eight to ten feet long. There is no substitute for it.

The advantages of a longeing cavesson over a halter should be discussed, lest it appear that nothing is lost in forgoing it. The nosepiece of the cavesson is reinforced with hinged metal plates, and the entire noseband is designed to buckle snugly in place. A swivel ring is at the center of the nosepiece, for attachment of the longeing tape. Thus, the longeing cavesson can be used both with more subtlety and more severity than a halter. The horse can feel the lightest signals from the trainer's hand.

When using a halter instead of a longeing cavesson, *the introductory lessons in longeing must be conducted in an enclosed area.* A paddock that is only slightly larger than the maximum size of the longeing circle is desirable. The enclosure is necessary to ensure control, because the horse, perplexed by the new work with a line and whip, is almost certain at some point to try to turn and bolt away. It will be very difficult to stop him with only a halter. Even when using a longeing cavesson, it is wise to start the longeing lessons in an enclosure. Many novice trainers have learned to their regret that, if a horse manages to bolt free once at the outset of training on the longe line, he will try it again and again. This is a problem not easily overcome, but if it is allowed to appear it has to be overcome before training can progress.

You may think that your horse will not be able to get away from you, even in an open field, if you use a longeing cavesson. After all, with the line snapped to the front of the nosepiece, you can yank him into a turn if he tries to run straight away from you. You don't have to try to outpull him, as you would with a halter. However, you must allow for the possibility that the line might become twisted around his neck when he wheels, or it might become entangled in his legs. There will be times when you must release the line for safety's sake.

Working in an enclosure has advantages in addition to preventionof escape. The walls are an aid in communicating to thehorse the idea of moving on a circle, and, as will be explained,they also can be used as an aid in stopping the horse, should hebecome headstrong on the circle.

Before starting the first lesson on the longe line, spend a fewminutes acquainting your horse with the whip. Show it to him,rub him with it, and move it about. If he is fearful when he sees itmoving, use the "sacking" technique to reassure him. Start with agentle lifting and swaying of the whip and build up to swinging iteasily over and around him. As a gesture to help build hisconfidence, do this: Whenever a swing of the whip startles thehorse, allow the lash to land very lightly on him, and then rubhim with the whip, as though you only intended to give him apleasant scratching. His fears of being hurt will gradually fade.

A whip is an indispensable aid in longeing a horse, because ineffect it lengthens the trainer's arm. It can be used to help guidethe horse, to urge him forward, and to check him. It can be used,if it ever becomes necessary, to punish aggressiveness. If it is usedintelligently, it will be respected by the horse, but it will not befeared as an unpredictable instrument of pain. Only a poor trainerproduces a horse that starts anxiously whenever he glimpses orhears a whip in motion.

First Longeing Lesson

Now, to proceed with the longeing lesson. The objectives in thisfirst session are to teach the horse to move on a circle around you,responding to voice commands to walk and halt. The sessionshould not last more than ten minutes. It is a mistake to tire ahorse when teaching him something new, for this lends an un-pleasant association to the experience, and working on a circle cantire even a well-trained horse within a short time.

Presuming that you are going to require the horse to move tothe left (counterclockwise) first, hold the longe line in your lefthand, with any extra length carefully coiled. If you allow a looseend to dangle at your feet, you are certain to trip on it, and may

be caught in it. Hold the whip in your right hand, with the butt
end toward the horse, and the lash trailing on the ground behind
you. This keeps the whip in an inconspicuous position when it is
not needed to help control the horse. With practice, you will become skillful at using wrist action to display the whip to the
horse, or crack it, with either hand.

If you are using a halter, the longe line should be snapped to
the ring on the left side. Later, when you longe the horse to the
right, the snap should be changed to the right side. This is prefer-
able to snapping the longe line to a ring underneath the jaw, particularly during early longeing lessons when the horse may pull
against the line, for it reduces the risk that the halter will be
twisted on the horse's head and rub against an eye.

Your biggest problem at the outset will be to "explain" to the
horse that he must move on the circle. Some trainers like to have
assistance in this step. Assistance is not necessary, particularly
when working in an enclosure, but it can simplify matters.

A trainer who has a helper stands in the center of the circle
while the assistant stands by the horse, his hand on the halter.
The trainer gives the voice command to "walk," and the assistant
sees to it that the horse responds correctly. At first, the assistant
holds the horse by the halter when walking. Then, as the horse
begins to move steadily, he releases the halter and merely accompanies the horse. Finally, he drops back and allows (or encourages) the horse to continue on the circle by itself. When all is
going well, the assistant steps out of the picture and the trainer
takes over the job of encouraging the horse to continue on the circle. If the horse hesitates, the whip is used to urge him on. Sometimes it is necessary to flick the horse lightly below the hocks;
sometimes all that is needed is a little snap of the whip.

When starting a horse on a circle without an assistant, use only
about ten feet of line at the beginning, to keep the horse within
easy reach of the whip. Position the horse so that he is facing the
direction he is to go, and then step back to your own position in
the center of the proposed circle. As you command the horse to
walk, extend the whip horizontally, pointing it toward his hocks.
If he does not start forward, flick the lash against his hocks, or
crack it. If you are lucky, the horse will discover immediately that
he is supposed to move on the circle. He may break into a trot or

canter, and may even race around the circle in excitement. Don't try to force him down to a walk. It is more important at this moment to allow him to move on the circle than to insist that he walk. However, do pay out the line smoothly to make the circle as large as possible. The faster he is moving, the more important it is to put him on a large circle, so that he will not injure his legs by twisting them. When he tires of moving at speed, he will slow down.

No doubt you noticed the phrase "If you are lucky" in the above paragraph. What do you do if the horse does not discover immediately that he is suppose to move on a circle? What if he simply turns and faces you, and tries to back away when you use the whip? Then it is up to you to make your instructions even clearer to him. Shorten the line until you are within two or three feet of him. Stand so that you are facing the left side of his neck. Then, with your left hand extended outward to your left as a "leading hand," encourage him to start forward, *and move on the circle with him*. The horse will be going forward on the circle, and you will be sidestepping, so that you can reach out with the whip (in your right hand) and touch his hindquarters when necessary to keep him moving. As the horse begins to walk steadily, gradually drop back to the center of the circle, paying out the line as you go. Whenever the horse hesitates or stops, move out to help him. Then return to the center of the circle.

If you would become expert at longeing horses, these are two rules that must be observed: 1. Never pull a horse off his track on a circle and bring him into the center for correction—always go to him, taking up slack in the line as you approach him. 2. Decide upon a specific spot as the center of your circle and *stay there*, except when deliberately moving out to help the horse.

Pulling a horse in to correct him is a mistake, because it gives him the idea of turning to face his handler in response to a tug on the longe line. In early work on the longe line, it is important for the horse to learn to remain on the track of his circle, facing his direction of movement, even when he comes to a halt. After this habit is firmly established, he may be taught to respond to a specific signal to turn and face his trainer, or to come in to him, or to proceed in the opposite direction; however, many trainers prefer never to include this in their schooling program.

Sometimes a horse, when learning work on the longe line, dis-

Preparation for ground driving Work on a circle on a longe line has many useful purposes. One of the lesser known advantages is that it can provide an introduction to ground driving. The equipment used may be simple or sophisticated. Gary Berke and Quarter Horse filly.

Step Two: longeing with two lines A horse that has been trained to work on a single longe line is now taught to move on the circle with two lines. The handler takes care not to permit either the horse or himself to become entangled in the lines. By crossing behind the horse, he can longe on a figure eight pattern.

Step three: ground driving Gradually, the trainer drops behind the horse, until he is no longer longeing, but ground driving. He stays a little off to one side, so he can easily swing the horse back into a longeing circle if there is trouble. Within a few days, he will introduce the horse to a bridle. When the time comes to start riding the young horse, he will understand how to respond to a bit.

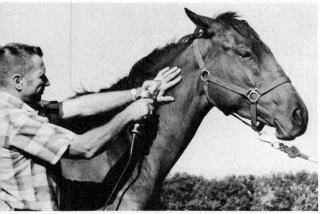

Resting clippers against his hand to let the young horse feel the vibration, Bob Black starts a lesson to acquaint the horse with the clippers. After a few moments, he will stroke the horse's neck with the humming instrument without actually clipping. Next, he will stroke the jaw, and then clip under the jaw. If the horse is extremely uneasy, the trainer will be satisfied to do only a little clipping every day, until all fear is gone. Three-year-old Quarter Horse filly, Holly, owned by the author. *Completely at ease about clippers* after several short daily sessions of training, the young horse permits the trainer to give his ears a touch-up. All horses are uneasy at first about handling of their ears. If their ears have been twisted and hurt by crude handlers, the training to accept clipping will require time and tact.

od technique in mane-pulling When it is *i*rable to shorten a horse's mane, as for rac- or jumping, the trainer should see to it that experience is not unpleasant or painful to horse. Working with one small strand of *r* at a time, the strand should be flattened *l* spread evenly between the teeth of a pulling *n*b, which has sharp edges between the *t*h. The end of the strand can be secured with *r*rap around the comb. Finally, the comb is *l*led downward with one smooth and easy *t*ion, the trainer's hand weighting the right *e* of the comb so that the comb cuts and pulls *m* right to left.

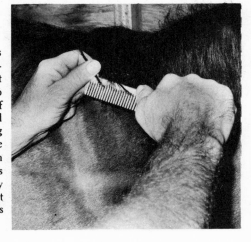

Standing in a cross-tie If a horse has been taught to stand tied with a single line, it is relatively easy to introduce cross-tying. The advantage of cross-tying is that it effectively prevents the horse from turning away from the handler. Here, Pat Richardson gives a bath to her four-year-old Arabian mare, Vinyard Merry Tez.

Trailer-loading a mildly stubb horse When a horse is stubb but not panicky or sullen, person alone can use a rump r to encourage him to ente trailer. The rump rope in this stance is a longe line, which been secured to the side of trailer. Its primary purpose is to force the horse into the trai but to prevent the horse fr backing away. If a horse is tremely difficult to load, at l one other persion should be p ent to assist. Susan English v Arabian gelding, Dawn O' L owned by Marty Nichols.

Training a Quarter Horse to Pose for the judges in conformation classes at shows, Kevin Nuckles is carefully attentive to the alignment of the legs. It takes many hours of work at home to condition a horse to respond correctly to cues to stand in good position and to hold the position. The horse also must learn to move well on straight lines at the walk and trot and exhibit cheerful good manners at all times. Kevin's horse is named Rutherford Scooter.

Leading a lonely life Horses are, by nature, gregarious creatures. They like to mingle with their own kind. In the civilized environment of mankind, however, the stallion that is owned by the nonprofessional horseman usually is segregated from other horses and is given little or no opportunity to breed mares. A stallion must be exercised regularly—play in a paddock is not sufficient. Otherwise, his pent-up energy and aggressiveness may be released in dangerous displays of ill temper. Arabian stallion Snow Eagle, photographed by his owner, Pearl O'Connell.

Showing a young horse the sights A practice called "ponying" is one of the best ways to introduce a young horse to the sights and sounds of the world in which he soon will be carrying a rider. Here, the author leads her two-year-old Thoroughbred gelding, Tradoc, away from his quiet rural environment to allow him to become accustomed to passing motorcars, to the shouts of children at play, barking dogs, and anything else that might be encountered during a ride. The "pony" being used for leading is not a pony at all in this instance. It is a sixteen-hand mule named Hazel, a strong, calm, benevolent baby-sitter owned by Dave and Sally Lamb. Photograph by Ransy Morr, courtesy of The Daily Press, Inc., Newport News-Hampton, Virginia.

Children often do better than adults in gaining the confidence of horses, because they are more casual. Here, Cindy Berke, by climbing up on a fence, actually is teaching a young horse not to fear the sight of a human towering overhead. This helps prepare the horse for his first lesson in being mounted.

Resting weight on the back of a young horse while brushing him is another way to help prepare him for his first lesson in being mounted. If a horse becomes accustomed to this, he is unlikely to panic just because someone slips onto his back. Horses that have had little or no handling before being ridden are instinctively fearful of anything they regard as an attack from above, because they are relatively defenseless against it.

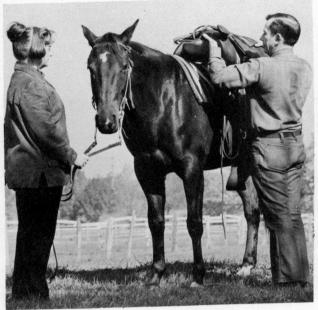

Good technique in saddling should be cultivated by all horse handlers. The saddle should be lifted and "settled" onto the horse's back with an air of easy confidence. If the handler is timid or harsh when saddling a young horse, he will make the horse anxious. His objective should be to teach the horse to stand perfectly still throughout the procedure. Here, Phyllis Fair holds the reins while her husband, Colonel Stan Fair, saddles their Quarter mare, Fox Lady.

Tightening the cinch or girth expertly can forestall the development of several bad habits that are so commonly found in horses. Whether working with a Western saddle or a flat saddle, the handler should do the job smoothly and swiftly. If he "fiddles" with the girth strap, jerking and tugging, the horse will become restless and resentful, and probably will learn to "puff up" in defense against the tightening. If the cinch is drawn too tight on a young horse, the horse may become panicky.

covers that he can interrupt the work as he pleases by stopping and wheeling to face his trainer, or by pivoting and darting in the opposite direction on the circle. This is a little game that only the horse enjoys. If your horse is at all clever, he will try it at least once. If you are clever, he will not try it more than once or twice. Correct him *instantly* by yanking hard on the longe line with your leading hand, and by simultaneously using the whip to put him back on the right track. If he starts backing away from you, let him go back until he encounters a wall of the enclosure. Then send him in the right direction with the whip.

Correction of a horse in a moment of rebellion always excites the horse. If this correction causes him to charge wildly around the circle, no matter. So long as he is going in the right direction, you have made your point. He will calm down, and will remember the lesson.

Some people become angry when a horse rebels. They resent it when they encounter problems in training their horses. They have not learned that it is only through the solving of problems that horses become trained. Good trainers enjoy coming to grips with challenges, for they know that challenges offer opportunities for real progress.

Although there are times when you will deliberately move toward your horse or away from him while working on the longe line, bear in mind that your object is to settle into one position and pivot there as the horse circles around you. A trainer who carelessly drifts around, unconsciously changing his position in response to tugs from the horse, never establishes a true circle for the horse. Your horse should learn the discipline of maintaining a true circle, staying as far from you as the length of the line permits, but keeping the line light in your hand. When the horse pulls against your hand, brace yourself and resist until he yields.

A horse that is pulling against the longe line while moving on a circle usually will not do it all the way around the circle. He will do it only on one part of the circle, probably at the point where he finds himself drawing near a gate, or where there are horses on the other side of the fence. When on the opposite side of the same circle, he will veer in, and the line will go slack in your hand. To prevent the horse from veering toward you, flick him on the shoulder with the whip.

Until you have developed dexterity in taking up slack in the line, you will find it difficult to keep it off the ground at all times. Occasionally, when the line goes down, the horse will step over it, and you will no longer be in control. All you can do is drop the line, and be grateful that you are working in an enclosed area where you can catch the horse by the halter.

After you have induced the horse to move around on the circle, and the initial excitement has faded, your immediate second task is to teach him to respond to signals to reduce pace and to stop. If he is trotting or cantering repeat your voice command to him to walk, and see if you can encourage him to do so by snapping the longe line downward several times, or by gently tugging at the line several times, taking care not to pull him off his track. If he does not understand, then say, "Whoa" or "Ho-o-o," whichever you prefer, and bring him to a complete halt by walking sideways to intercept him on his track, taking up the slack in the line as you approach him. If you do this calmly and smoothly, it should not upset him. At any rate, once he has halted, let him stand and rest for a little while as a reward for his work.

It won't take the horse long to learn that when you start moving sideways to intercept him on his track you intend to stop him. As soon as he grasps this, if you are succeeding in cultivating an attitude of obedience he will start slowing down whenever he sees you stepping sideways. Soon, your voice alone, or your voice assisted by a little snap downward on the longe line, will slow or halt him.

Sometimes, due to excitement, a horse becomes headstrong on a circle, increasing pace and trying to pull away instead of slowing down as the trainer approaches to stop him. If this occurs with your horse, gradually change your position until you are longeing the horse quite close to a wall of the enclosure. Make your move to intercept him as he approaches the wall, so that the wall will block any attempt to pull away. If the enclosure in which you are working is square-cornered, all the better. Guide the horse into a corner and stop him. Then give a pat to reassure him that all is well, and allow him to regain his composure before putting him back to work.

Although your objectives in this first session are to teach the horse to move on a circle around you, responding to voice commands to walk and halt, feel free to change the objectives in accordance with the progress of your horse. You may decide to be satisfied with less, if the horse is tiring, or you may decide to ask a little more, if you have encountered no real difficulties. It may well be that the only positive thing the horse learns in the first session is to move on a circle. Perhaps you are not sure that the horse understands the voice commands to walk and to halt. Rather than pursue the work with a tired pupil, wait until the next day to concentrate on the voice commands. However, if your horse takes the introductory lesson calmly, and even seems to prefer walking to moving at the faster gaits, you can try teaching him the word "trot" as well as the word "walk."

The horse should be taught to circle in both directions during the first session if possible. A horse that is worked only in one direction for one or two sessions will stubbornly resist later attempts to make him go the other way. He will think that he has found the "right way" to circle on the longe line. You must see to it that your horse develops no preferences.

Whenever you want to turn the horse to reverse directions, stop him first, then go to him and turn him around. Remember that you do not want him to pick up the idea of turning to face you when he halts. If you plan to teach him to reverse directions in response to a voice command, wait until he has become proficient in satisfying other requirements.

How can you know when your horse has reached the limit of the amount of physical work he should perform in a longeing session? Here is a simple guide to follow: When the horse's body becomes warm and *slightly moist* with sweat, he has had enough work. Horses do not become as hot and wet with sweat on a longe line as they do when being ridden, unless they are greatly excited, but this does not mean that they do not become tired. The work on circles places heavy demands on their legs.

Voice Commands

Over a period of several days, or within two weeks at most, you should be able to teach your horse to walk, trot, and halt by voice commands. After he has learned these commands, teach him to canter on command. Finally, if you desire to do so, you can teach him to reverse directions on command.

Some horsemen think the words "walk" and "trot" may be confusingly similar to horses, because they are both of one syllable. They recommend adding another word to one of the commands. A trainer, can, for instance, say, "Walk," and add the horse's name. Other trainers, however, never encounter any problems in teaching a horse to distinguish between one-syllable words. Perhaps it is because they use a different tone of voice with each command. They usually say, "Walk," rather gently, and "Trot" rather sharply.

Regardless of the words or intonations you use, speak softly when giving commands. Raise your voice only enough to be heard by your horse. If the horse does not obey, either because he is confused or because he is stubborn, shouting at him would be an exercise in futility. It is poor policy, even, to repeat a command several times before requiring a horse to obey it. If you order a horse to halt, and he does not comply, repeat the order once, to be certain he has heard it. Then, if he fails to halt, *take action to compel him to halt.* Trainers who say, "Whoa" a dozen times while their horses continue to move heedlessly on a longeing circle are not disciplinarians in any sense of the word.

When a horse is first learning a word of command and its meaning, he cannot be expected to obey it the instant he hears it. He has to make a conscious response. Therefore, when you give him an order, allow him several seconds to translate it into action. If you watch him carefully, you will be able to see signs that he has heard the command and is trying to decide what to do. If he is standing still, he will stiffen perceptibly, or if he is moving, his pace will falter. After a moment, he may relax, or the hesitancy may disappear, indicating that he has stopped thinking about the order. At that moment, you should repeat the order or take action to require compliance.

With practice a horse will learn a voice command so well that he no longer has to make a conscious response. The instant he hears the command he will obey it. You will know then that the response is a conditioned reflex.

Teach your horse to respond to a cluck of the tongue when you want him to move more energetically at a gait. It would only confuse him to try to urge him on by telling him to "walk" when he is already walking, or to "trot" when he is already trotting. Simply cluck your tongue, then snap your whip. It is an easy signal for him to learn, and it will be useful later when you start line-driving lessons.

To reward a horse for responding correctly to a command, simply say, "Good" or any other word of praise you want him to learn, and do not give him another command for a while. If you have required him to walk, allow him to walk around the circle two or three times. If you have stopped him, allow him to stand quietly for a minute or so. Reward is not necessarily cessation of work, but cessation of pressure, which in this case is the pressure of learning new things.

Trainers who cannot resist giving commands in rapid succession often succeed only in bewildering and antagonizing their horses. To the horses, it must seem that the trainers are never pleased with anything. Allowing a horse to go around a circle several times at a given pace reassures him that he is doing the right thing.

You may have difficulty in teaching your horse to canter on the longe line. Urging him into the canter may excite him, and if he attempts to pull away it will be harder to hold him than at the walk or trot. Here again, the fact that you are working in an enclosure will save the day.

The first few times that the horse responds correctly to the command to canter, do not be concerned about his leads, and do not try to insist that he hold the canter for more than a few strides. If he is pulling against the longe line at the moment he strikes off into the canter, he probably will take the wrong lead. And whether his lead is right or wrong, he probably will canter only briefly before breaking to a trot. Let him trot around the circle once or twice and settle down before asking him to canter again. If your attitude is one of helpfulness instead of exasperation, you will find that each time he tries the canter he will be calmer about it, and as he becomes calm he will start taking the correct lead, and will hold the gait longer with only a little urging.

When your horse works lightly in hand at all gaits, you can teach him to reverse directions at your command. For this, when using a halter, the longe line should be snapped under the halter.

Always bring the horse to a halt before ordering him to reverse. When he halts, change the line and the whip in your hands. Then give the command "Reverse" or "Change," and tug on the line to suggest that he turn around. Extend the whip to block any attempt to proceed in the wrong direction, and crack it, if necessary, to encourage him to turn around and go the other way.

Principles of Exercising

A horse that has learned the fundamentals of longeing can be given carefully regulated exercise. His work always should be started on large circles, and he should be warmed up with a walk, just as he will be warmed up later when being ridden. No matter how fresh and frolicsome he feels at the beginning of a session, be firm with him about walking. Some trainers allow their horses to frisk around to work off excess energy before settling to work. This is the easiest thing to do, but it is not good for the horse to chase around in circles before warming up properly.

Is it "fair" to ask a horse to settle down and behave himself when he is feeling frolicsome? It certainly is, if you intend to have a well-disciplined horse. Some people sound almost as though they are boasting when they say that their horses get "high" and hard to handle when they have been kept in for a few days, or when the weather is cold. They seem to take it for granted that high spirits and misbehavior go together. However, as an old horseman once said, "A broke horse should behave himself even when he feels like exploding. If he doesn't, then he isn't really broke."

After a horse is warmed up on a large circle on the longe line, the size of the circle can be reduced. While the horse is trotting, *gradually* shorten the longe line, so that the horse slowly spirals inward. The smaller the circle becomes, the more difficult it will be for the horse to move in good balance, so do not ask too much at first. You will know the horse is having a problem when he starts pulling against the line. This will mean that he has not shifted his balance back far enough to enable him to use or "engage" the hindquarters effectively to lift and drive himself into the smaller circle. (Horses are rear-engined animals.) Do not reduce the size of the circle further—concentrate on resisting the pulling, and on keeping the horse moving at the trot. Let the horse discover how to solve the problem. When the horse finds his balance, the line will become light in your hand. As a reward, gradually pay out the line, enlarging the circle. Then repeat the exercise in the opposite direction. From day to day, you will find that the horse can move comfortably into smaller and smaller circles. It is enough for him to learn to maintain the trot and the canter for brief periods on circles about twenty feet in diameter.

When you are exercising your horse or schooling him on the longe line, give him equal work in both directions. Working him only in one direction would make him "one-sided." Can you imagine a weight-lifter exercising only one arm?

At this point in training on the longe line, you may be tempted to put your horse into a bitting harness to start teaching him collection, particularly if you have a Saddlebred colt, or if you have a Western type colt and live in an area where there is a lot of talk about "setting a horse's head." This is unnecessary, and may even do more harm than good, if you plan to give your horse sound basic training at his natural gaits. Teaching a horse to collect or "gather" himself belongs in a later stage of schooling.

Introducing Line-Driving

Instead of working toward collection, now is the time to use longeing as a means of introducing the horse to line-driving.

For driving, you will need two longe lines, and a longeing cavesson, or a halter. Halters are not ideal for driving, because horses are inclined to ignore them when they become headstrong. However, if your horse is well trained at longeing, you will be able to use one. The rope halter is suggested because it can act with a little more severity than a leather halter.

Even though you may have a driving bridle with a bit, it should not be used in the early driving lessons. There is too much risk of hurting the horse's mouth in moments of excitement. Introducing a horse to a bit for driving and riding will come later. The technique is described in Chapter IX.

It should hardly be necessary to suggest that the early lessons in driving be conducted inside an enclosure. Unless you have handled driving lines before, it is going to be difficult for you at first. Keeping the slack out of the lines, so that the horse will not step over them, will be a problem. As in longeing, whenever the horse becomes entangled in a line, the safest thing to do is to drop it.

Above all, watch your own footwork to be certain that *you* do not step over a line accidentally and become entangled in it.

When you are ready to start the first driving lesson, fasten both lines to the longeing cavesson or to the bosal or halter. If you are using a cavesson, fasten the lines to the side rings. If you are using a bosal or halter, secure the lines underneath. With your hands on two lines, you should be able to prevent the bosal headstall or the halter from displacing.

Your first step will be to longe the horse, with one line (the inside line) in your leading hand as usual, and the other line passed around the outside of the horse and held in your hand that normally carries the whip. As the horse is longed, the outside line should rest lightly above the hocks. With practice, you will discover just how much tension is needed to keep it in position.

Before starting the horse on the longeing circle, stand by his halter and loop the outside line around his hindquarters. If you sacked the horse in his earlier handling, he should not be afraid of the line while standing still. Be prepared, however, for him to be startled by the feel of the line when he begins to move.

Try to start the horse at a walk, but don't be concerned if he goes faster. If he breaks into a canter or even bolts around the circle, give him as much line as you can, and let him move. After a few laps, he will realize that the line around his hindquarters is not hurting him, and he will slow down. Then you can take control of his pace.

The outside line gives you an added control that you did not have in ordinary longeing. With it, you can easily prevent the horse from turning to face you. If he starts to turn his head inward or swing his hindquarters out, you have only to tighten the outside line to keep him on his track. Occasionally, while you are learning to handle the lines, you may accidentally allow the outside line to slip up onto the horse's back. When this happens, stop the horse, go to him, and return the line to its correct position.

If you have a driving harness or surcingle, you can let the horse wear it to become accustomed to it during his early driving lessons, but *do not* run the lines through any rings or loops attached to the harness. The rings or loops would keep the lines from slipping out of position, but it is important now to be able to use the lines freely for longeing as well as for driving. You will soon see that whenever the horse becomes headstrong in driving you can regain control quickly by returning him to a longeing circle.

Some trainers say they like to put Western saddles on their young horses, tie the stirrups down, and run the driving lines through the stirrups to keep them in place. This also is something that should not be done in the introductory driving lessons. In fact, there is little to recommend the practice at any stage of driving training. It won't take you long to learn to keep the lines in position.

Assuming now that you are longeing your horse on a circle to the left, and that he has lost any initial fear of the line around his hindquarters, put him into a walk. Then take a few steps toward his hindquarters and start walking on a small circle inside the circle he is making, half longeing and half driving him.

When you first shift your position and start walking inside the horse's circle, with the horse slightly in the lead, the horse probably will be more puzzled than frightened. Encourage him to go on, and, if necessary, flip the outside driving line against his hindquarters. When he is moving steadily, start making the circle larger, dropping back until the horse is definitely ahead of you, although you are still to the left of his track. Don't take up a position directly behind the horse. By staying to the left you can easily counter trouble by returning him to a longeing circle. For safety's sake, *keep the lines long enough to assure that you are out of "kicking range."* You may feel you can trust your horse not to kick, but this is a new experience for him. He might be startled into kicking at the lines, and injure you by mistake.

When your circle becomes so large that you have reached the limits of the enclosure in which you are working, drive him around to the left inside the enclosure. Then gradually return to a longeing-size circle, and shift back to longeing instead of driving. Stop the horse, and let him rest.

The next step is simple: Repeat the above exercise, in the opposite direction. Then let the horse quit work for the day.

You will have noted that the first lesson does not include teaching the horse to halt in response to a signal from the lines. The reason for this is that you should not try to stop the horse with the lines while you are walking to the right or left of his track. In attempting to do so, you would cause him to shift his hindquarters to one side. In the first lesson, whenever you are driving and want to halt the horse, use a voice command. If he does not obey the voice command, return him to a longeing circle and stop him.

In the horse's second driving lesson, if you feel that he is doing well, you can start teaching him to turn and halt in response to signals from the lines.

To introduce turning, drive through figure eights that are as large as the enclosure permits. Each time you reach a point where you are to change directions, *cross over behind the horse* and guide him into the new direction, encouraging him to maintain pace as he turns.

In early driving lessons, all turns should be easy and gradual. If you try to demand sharp turns before the horse is ready for them, he may develop a habit of "rubbernecking." This means he will always bend his neck sideways before turning, and this is a major fault, because it prevents him from learning to turn in good balance.

After the horse has learned a little about turning, start teaching him to halt in response to the lines.

When you are ready to ask him to halt, step into a position directly behind him. Walk a few steps with him, and then simply slow down and stop, setting your hands to resist his forward movement. Don't try to *pull* him to a halt. Let him feel that he has encountered a barrier—that he has come "to the end of the lines," so to speak. This is the same technique that you used to stop him when you taught him to halt while being led at halter. You allowed the horse to discover that, when he yielded to your fixed and resisting hand by stopping, the lead line became light, because *you* were not doing the pulling. If he learned that lesson well, this one should be no problem.

By the third driving lesson, you should be able to take the horse outside the enclosure for his schooling. His response to the signals to turn can be improved by driving him around and between objects such as bushes and trees. His response to the signal to halt can be improved, not by worrying him with frequent stops and starts, but by stopping him occasionally and allowing him to enjoy a brief recess from work.

How Much Should You Drive?

How much training in line-driving should a young horse be given? At present, your only purpose in teaching the horse to drive is to help prepare him for the experience of being ridden. The better he responds to your commands to go forward, turn, and halt, and the more accustomed he is to the discipline of work, the easier it will be to handle him once you are on his back. It is up to you to decide how much practice he should have.

In addition to teaching the horse to maneuver in response to the driving lines, you may want to use driving to give him some cross-country experience. You can drive him away from his familiar surroundings, go up and down hills, over ditches, across bridges, and even through water if you don't mind getting your feet wet.

Both you and the horse will enjoy the sightseeing trips, and the bond of trust between you will grow. The horse will learn that he must go wherever you tell him to go, even though he may be fearful because he is leading the way. If you take care to see that he comes to no harm, you will be teaching him to have faith in your judgment.

What should you do when the horse balks at going over something that frightens him? Let's say, for instance, that you want him to step over a fallen log, and he is afraid to do it. He balks, snorts, and starts to draw back and turn away from it. Be cool about it. Don't try to drive him forcefully over the log, but use all the skill you can muster to keep him from turning away from it.

Require him to stand facing the log and gently, repeatedly, and persistently encourage him to go on. Don't be in a hurry. If it takes the horse five minutes to decide to go on, it is worth the wait. What if he does not decide to go on? He will, when you convince him that you are not going to give up. He will gain confidence from the apparent fact that you are unexcited and quite sure of yourself, and he also will become rather bored with the idea of staying in one place so long.

Every time you drive the horse over an obstacle that he questions, and he finds that none of his fears are realized, you score a decisive gain in your quest for his total confidence. There is nothing quite like the feeling of satisfaction you will have as a trainer when the time comes that the horse will go anywhere, over anything, with little or no hesitation because he knows that you are holding the lines.

CHAPTER VIII

Trailer Training

In theory, all young horses should receive trailer training as part of their early schooling program. Before there is any need to transport them anywhere, they should learn to walk into trailers quietly, ride in them quietly, and step out of them quietly. In reality, most horses receive no trailer training until their owners want to take them on a trip. Sometimes there is no harm done. Horses can learn to do by doing, particularly if their handlers know what they are doing. Sometimes, however, there is much harm done. Horses can turn into "problem loaders" very quickly when unskilled handlers, under pressure of travel schedules, become exasperated at delays and resort to force without discretion.

If you are inexperienced at loading horses, and have a horse that needs to be trained or retrained to go into trailers, it would be well to set aside some time to work with him before the necessity for travel arises. Daily trailer training for a week would be beneficial to both you and the horse. However, this may be impractical. Perhaps you do not have a trailer, and hesitate to borrow one. If you cannot give your horse advance training, at least promise yourself that when the time comes to load the horse for a trip you will allow ample time to work with him carefully and correctly.

Now for a word of warning: Beware of volunteers who want to help you load your horse. You will find that, whenever you appear to have trouble loading a horse for a trip, people will offer assistance. They may or may not be qualified to help. Some people will not only volunteer but insist on helping by clucking to your horse or waving their arms. They may even try to take the horse out of your hands. Don't be one bit timid. Tell them in no uncertain terms that you do not want their help. You can be sure that the overbearing volunteers are not knowledgeable horsemen, for no horseman worthy of the name would start helping without your express invitation.

A second person can give useful assistance to you in working with a recalcitrant horse, even though he is relatively inexperienced, if he is willing to listen to your instructions and do only as you ask. And there certainly is no reason not to accept help from an expert, if you approve of his methods. In helping you, the expert will give you a valuable demonstration of the technique in loading a horse.

Every expert has his own favorite way of working with a horse that is stubborn about loading. An old-timer may snap a whip repeatedly at the heels of a horse, to irritate him just enough to cause him to step into the trailer to escape the stinging. Another old-timer may prefer to swat the horse harmlessly with the flat side of a kitchen broom to startle him into going into the trailer. When methods such as these are employed by experts, there is little or no risk that the horse will suffer from the experience. When they are employed crudely, however, they can excite a horse into a desperate struggle and may cause him to be injured. To be on the safe side, never permit anyone to use such methods on your horse unless you know him and have every reason to trust his skill.

More commonly, now, horsemen use ropes around the hindquarters of their horses to overcome problems in loading. Their techniques may vary somewhat, but if they know what they are doing they work on the same principle: *They do not use the ropes to force their horses to move forward, but to prevent them from stepping backward.* If you ever see anyone trying to use a rope to force a horse bodily into a trailer, you will know he is no expert with the rope.

Techniques with ropes will be described in detail in this chapter. They are easier to learn than the techniques of using whips or brooms. The latter require near-perfect timing, which can be acquired through practice, but the cost would be too high if you made mistakes at the expense of your horse while learning.

Loading the Unspoiled Horse

If your young horse is unspoiled about loading into trailers, you probably will not need to use ropes in his training. By sacking, longeing, and line-driving him, you have won his confidence and respect to such an extent that he may walk into a trailer with only your words for encouragement.

Plan your first loading session carefully. Use only a solidly built trailer, with the hitch secured to a car or other object, so that the trailer is level and will not tip backward or forward. Horses are extremely wary of stepping onto anything that feels insubstantial. The trailer should be a two-horse model, so that you can safely enter with the horse if necessary—you can enter on one side of the center partition, guiding the horse into the other side. It should be roomy in height, width, and length. The higher the ceiling, the better. A green horse will not bump his head when *entering* a low-ceilinged trailer, but he is likely to do so when he *backs out,* because his head will rise when his hind legs step down.

Arrange for the horse to be a little hungry for grain at the time of the loading session. Place some grain in the tray inside the trailer. It will be his "instant reward" for entering the trailer.

In addition to the usual halter shank, have an extra-long lead line at hand. A line ten or twelve feet long will do, or you can use a longeing tape.

Before taking the horse to the trailer, open the trailer doors wide, and make certain that there are no protruding latches that might cause injury. Open any front windows, to give the trailer an airy atmosphere.

If there are any spectators, caution them ahead of time not to crowd around the horse or attempt to help unless you ask for assistance. Assure them that you are in no hurry to load the horse.

Using the extra-long lead line, lead the horse straight toward the entry door of the trailer. If the horse becomes anxious, and turns sideways as you reach the entry, make nothing of it. Stop there, as though you intended merely to walk to the trailer and rest a bit. After the horse relaxes, step into the trailer, leaving the horse at the doorway (on the long lead line), and walk nonchalantly to the front of the trailer and rustle the grain in the feed tray. Make certain that the horse notices the feed, and realizes where it is, even if you have to take a little to him in your hand and then rustle the grain in the tray again.

Next, step back out of the trailer, and exchange the long lead line for the short one. Lead the horse away from the trailer, walking by his left shoulder, then start straight toward the door again. Your intent is to conduct a test. Although it is not likely, it is possible that the horse will voluntarily enter the trailer by himself. As you approach the trailer door, put the lead rope over the horse's neck, and lead him with your hand at the halter ring. At the slightest hesitation of the horse at the door, cluck to him reassuringly. If he starts into the trailer by himself, release your hold on the halter—but be prepared to reach for the line if he changes his mind and backs out. If the horse goes all the way into the trailer, quickly snap the guard chain into place behind him, or close the trailer door, to prevent him from backing out.

Chances are slim that the horse will voluntarily enter the trailer alone this early in his training. Try him only one or two times— no more. Don't turn the experiment into an argument.

If the horse does not enter the trailer, replace the short lead line with the long one, and then walk into the trailer yourself, leaving the horse at the door (unless, of course, he decides to enter with you). Do not walk in on the same side of the partitioned trailer that the horse is to enter, unless there is a safe exit for you at the front.

Now, assuming that you are in the trailer and the horse has not followed, you are going to play a waiting game. Do you remember how, when line-driving, you handled your horse when he was afraid to step over an obstacle? You did not try to force him over the obstacle, but you did not permit him to turn away from it. After the horse was convinced that you were not going to become excited and were not going to give up, he stepped over the obstacle. You will use the same technique to induce him to enter the trailer. It will be helpful to have an assistant now, *not* to try to urge the horse to enter the trailer, but to stand ready to move in and close the door behind the horse.

With chucking signals on the lead line, and perhaps a little rattling of the grain in the feed tray, encourage the horse to come into the trailer. Do not pull on the halter line, because it will not work, and it will only arouse a stubborn attitude. The unspoiled horse hesitates to enter a trailer because he is anxious about it, not because he is deliberately being stubborn. Even though you do not pull on the line, however, persist in giving the horse encouragement to enter. Don't let him simply stand at the door and look around at the scenery.

After a minute, or a few minutes, the horse may tentatively start into the trailer. Perhaps he will step into it with both forefeet, then stop, then back out. It is an experiment on his part. He wants to know what you will do about it when he backs out. Do not try to hold him in the trailer. Use the lead line only to keep him from turning away or backing away from the trailer *after* he has stepped out. Then encourage him to enter the trailer again.

The horse may make three or four false starts before he finally decides to walk all the way into the trailer. As soon as he is inside, your helper should close the door behind him.

This process may require ten or fifteen minutes. It will never require that much time again. You have induced the horse to enter the trailer voluntarily, and you have given him not the slightest cause to fear a repetition of the experience.

Using Ropes in Loading

Will this coaxing technique be effective with any and all young horses? What about a colt that has not yet been gentled? Or one that has been gentled but is stubborn about loading because of bad experiences in the past? By all means, try the technique, but don't count on success. An untamed colt cannot be expected to trust you. Even the young horse that you have gentled and trained to longe and drive is unlikely to trust you about trailers, if he has had trouble with them before. Given any choice at all, he will choose not to co-operate. You will have to convince him that he has no choice. You can do this by using ropes, or your longeing or driving lines, if they are strong.

A horseman who is skilled in using ropes or lines to load horses can handle almost any "problem loader," no matter how violently or sullenly the horse resists. You will need practice to become skilled, but your experience in handling lines in longeing and driving will make the process much easier for you than for the average person.

As your horse already is accustomed to the feel of lines around his hindquarters, it will not be necessary to take time out from your loading session to acquaint him with it. However, in the case of a horse that is skittish about ropes or lines, spend a few minutes longeing and leading him with a line looped around his hindquarters. It is *not* your intent to use the lines to frighten the horse into the trailer.

If you are going to use ropes rather than longeing tapes, they should be at least one half inch in diameter. The smaller they are, the more easily they can cut into a horse if tested violently. Soft nylon or cotton ropes are better than lariats, because they are unlikely to inflict burns by abrasion.

The simplest and safest technique calls for two helpers, a long lead shank, and two ropes or lines about twenty-five feet in length. The long lines will be used to make a "chute" through which the horse will be led into the trailer. Fasten them to the trailer at the door where the horse is to enter (you can snap them to the rings that support the rear-guard chain). You and one of your helpers each can handle one of the long lines. Step back from the trailer and draw the lines tight to make the chute. The third person's task is to lead the horse through the chute and into the trailer. If the horse is fearful of entering the chute, widen it until he is in it and then close in. As soon as possible, cross behind the horse, exchanging places with the helper who is holding the other line. With the lines crossed behind the horse, above his hocks, you will be able to prevent the hindquarters from swinging sideways as the horse advances toward the trailer. You also will be able to counter attempts by the horse to back up.

Explain carefully to the person who is leading the horse that his only job is to guide the horse and keep his head straight. *He is not to try to pull the horse toward the trailer at any time. If he forgets and pulls on the halter, he will cause the horse to intensify his efforts of resistance.* You and the other helper, working from behind, will be entirely responsible both for inducing the horse to go forward, and for preventing him from backing.

To induce the horse to step forward in the chute, tighten the crossed lines around his hindquarters enough to make him distinctly uncomfortable, and then *wait for him to step forward to find relief from the pressure.* Do not try to force him bodily toward the trailer. Wait for him to move, even if it takes several minutes. The instant he steps forward, relax the pressure without dropping the lines, and allow him to stand quietly for a few moments. Then apply pressure again to ask for another step. When he complies, relax the lines again. Do this repeatedly, preventing any attempts by the horse to swing sideways or back up. Don't be concerned if it takes time to move the horse all the way to the trailer door, for the horse is being "educated" to the use of the lines at every step.

Upon reaching the trailer door, the helper who is leading the horse should enter the trailer and move forward. Now, he must be particularly careful to keep the horse's head straight.

At this point the horse may enter the trailer without further difficulty. Or he may start to enter the trailer and then change his mind. He may decide to make one final big test of the strength of the crossed lines behind him, and throw his weight backward. Two persons with crossed lines ordinarily can prevent a horse from going backward. When they do, the horse probably will decide his struggles are useless, and enter the trailer.

Sometimes, in pitching his weight backward, a horse loses his footing and starts to fall. If this happens, release the lines to reduce the possibility that the horse will become entangled. However, as soon as the horse starts to regain his footing, return the lines to their position and be ready to ask him anew to enter the trailer. Don't give him a second's delay.

No one likes to see a horse fall, but the experience can have a sobering effect on an unruly animal. If you can work quickly enough to put him into the trailer immediately after the fall, he may well be "cured" of his loading problem forever after. If, however, you give him even a few minutes' rest after the fall, he may become more troublesome than before. He may become more afraid of loading . . . or he may decide that falling paid off handsomely. Horses *can* learn that they can win respite by throwing themselves down.

The loading technique described above can be modified if you do not have two helpers.

If you have one helper, you can run a line from the horse's halter into the trailer, through the tie ring at the feed tray, and back out again. Then you can handle both the lead line and one of the lines around the hindquarters.

Working Without Assistance

If you have no helpers, you can do the job alone, but it is somewhat dangerous for a novice. Before taking the horse up to the trailer, put the long lead line in place in the trailer, ready for use. Fasten another long line to the right side of the trailer doorway. Then lead the horse to the trailer and snap the long lead line to his halter. Pass the other line around his hindquarters. Using your left hand to guide the horse, and your right hand to work with the line around the hindquarters, apply pressure to the hindquarters to "ask" the horse to step forward. Work with the horse as described previously. Apply pressure, and wait for him to yield to it. Then apply pressure again to ask for another step. As soon as the horse's head is inside the trailer, but before his forefeet have stepped into it, prepare for the big test of the line that the horse will make if he starts to enter and then changes his mind. As you probably will not be strong enough to hold the horse if he pitches backward violently, pass a fold of the long line around a sturdy part of the trailer, such as the center supporting post if you are loading the horse to the right of the post. One wrap of the fold around the post is sufficient to meet the test if the horse starts backward. Do not tie the line, for you will want to unwrap it quickly if the horse starts to fall. *And be absolutely certain that your hand or fingers cannot become caught in the line.*

As stated earlier, it is safest to have two helpers when using lines to load a horse. There is less risk that anyone will get a hand caught. The most common injury suffered by individuals in loading horses is a hand injury. Not long ago, I met a man whose left hand was encased in a cast. He said two fingers were almost amputated when they were caught in a line that was wrapped around a post as a horse went backward. I expressed sympathy, then added, philosophically, that I doubted that he ever would let it happen again. At that he showed me his other hand. The middle finger was grotesquely crooked. "I sure hope I've learned my lesson," he said, "because this happened last year when I was loading a horse, and I'm running out of fingers."

One thing to remember for the sake of the horse is to keep the hindquarters line over his tail if possible. A line that accidentally slips up high under the dock of the tail frightens most horses, and may cause severe burns or deep cuts in moments of violence.

Handling the Sullen Horse

Even though there can be a lot of action when a horse becomes violent, experienced horsemen agree that violent horses are easier to load than sullen horses. The truly sullen horse usually arouses anger in people who try to handle him, because he does not appear to be afraid of the trailer, but he balks at the trailer door and will not budge. He will endure any kind of punishment with a stolidity that is almost beyond human understanding.

Sullen horses *can* be understood by people who are sensitive enough to realize that they are pathetic creatures—perhaps the most pathetic of all horses that have been mishandled by inept trainers. They have been conditioned into the abnormality of accepting pain and suffering without reaction to it. In any situation involving handling by people, they have lost that spark of life that should cause them to seek escape from harm.

If you are faced with the problem of loading a sullen horse into a trailer, you can be sure that it is worse than useless to inflict punishment for balking. Active punishment will only cause him to sink into an unresponsive stupor. You will have to *avoid* giving him the impression that you are doing anything to punish him. What can you do? You can use the same long-line technique that you can use with any other horse, allowing for the fact that more time and patience will be required. If you take the time necessary, and get the job done, you will have initiated a process of retraining that eventually will result in a horse that loads easily. This does not mean that the horse will be restored to normal, in that his tendency to "sulk" under pressure will disappear, but it does mean that he will learn to walk into trailers.

It might be helpful to describe an actual case of a sullen horse. The owner asked me one day if I would assist him in loading the horse for a trip. He said he had bought the horse a year earlier, and enjoyed riding it, although it had "balky spells." However, he had never been able to load it into a trailer. He knew a little of the background of the horse, including the fact that the previous owners had once become so angry about his resistance to loading that they had used a tractor to literally drag him into a trailer. They had run a heavy rope through a front opening in the trailer, secured it to the horse, and hauled him inside. Of course, there were injuries. Fortunately they were not severe.

For our loading session, I asked the owner to handle the lead shank, and explained that I would work behind the horse with a long line. My line was a nylon rope. In this instance, I preferred not to have a helper working with me behind the horse. The owner had no difficulty in leading the horse up to the trailer door. It was there that the horse always balked. The owner stepped into the left aisle of the trailer, prepared to guide the horse into the right aisle. I fastened the long line to the right side of the door that the horse was to enter, then drew the line around behind the horse and up to the left side of the door. As I wrapped the line around the center supporting pole, I drew the line *as tightly as possible* against the hindquarters of the horse. I secured the line with a double wrap around the pole, for I knew there would be a long wait for the horse to move, and I didn't care to tire myself by trying to hold the horse's weight.

It was a long wait. The horse, instead of stepping forward to relieve the pressure of the rope around the hindquarters, simply sat back against it. That was all right with me, for it made the rope even tighter, and the longer he sat against it the more uncomfortable it would become. Yet it would be plain to the horse that I was not actively urging him to go forward. I engaged the owner in casual conversation to pass the time. It was perhaps ten minutes before I saw the horse stir a little, experimentally shifting his weight forward and backward to find out what would happen. I made no move to indicate my interest. Finally, cautiously, the horse eased an inch or so forward, just enough to slacken the line and keep it slack. Still I showed no interest. I continued to chat with the owner for two or three minutes. Then, nonchalantly, I drew the line tight again, secured it, and continued my conversation with the owner.

The progress we made was slow but sure. At no point did the horse suddenly decide to give up and walk voluntarily into the trailer. The process required more than an hour, not because there was any great distance to cover, but because of the long waits between steps. Yet we did succeed.

As it turned out, the horse was almost as difficult to unload as to load. To require him to back out of the trailer, we used a line across his chest to ask him to step backward, one step at a time.

From that time on, the owner used the same technique to load and unload the horse. The second time the horse was loaded, the process required about twenty minutes. The third time, it took five minutes. After that, the horse would go into a trailer without delay. However, he never learned to load without a rope around his hindquarters. The line seemed to give him a sense of security. The owner didn't mind.

Ordinarily, in the training of horses, it is desirable to use long lines only in the introductory loading lessons. As soon as possible, horses should be encouraged to walk into trailers without assistance. The best-trained horses walk confidently into trailers by themselves, allowing their handlers to stay behind to close the doors.

After you have loaded your young horse for the first time, and closed the door behind him, tie his halter rope so that he cannot twist sideways in the trailer, and allow him to eat the grain in the feed tray. Then give him some hay, and take him for a drive if possible. Travel several miles, to acquaint him with the sensation of riding in a trailer. Take care not to let this turn into a bad experience. If for any reason the horse finds it difficult to keep his footing during his first few rides, he may become jittery about hauling. Be certain that the flooring of the trailer is not conducive to slipping. And drive smoothly, accelerating and reducing speed gradually, and slowing to five miles an hour for right-angle turns.

Watch ahead for drivers on side roads who may decide to pull out in front of you, heedless of the fact that you are towing a horse trailer. Sudden braking can send your horse to his knees. On dusty roads, drive slowly. Horses have been suffocated by dust rolling into trailers from behind.

Tips on Unloading

When you stop to unload the horse, allow him to stand in the trailer a little while before taking him out. Don't let him get the idea that he is supposed to be unloaded immediately upon stopping. If the weather is warm, see that the horse has adequate ventilation by opening the front vents or windows and one or both of the rear trailer doors, leaving the guard chains fastened.

The first thing you must do when preparing to unload the horse is to untie his halter rope. Do this *before* unfastening the rear-guard chain, or before opening the rear door if there is no guard chain. This is extremely important, because if the horse starts backing out of the trailer while he is still tied, and comes to the end of the halter rope after his hind feet are on the ground, he will panic and either break the halter or injure himself in a desperate struggle. From then on, he will be fearful when he backs out of a trailer, and will always exit in a great rush.

You must try to see to it that the horse exits slowly the first time and every time that you unload him during his trailer training. After you untie the halter rope, go to the rear of the trailer and quietly open the door and let down the guard chain. Then step in beside the horse and give him a pat. Do not ask him to start back immediately. Just hope that he will wait for you to give him a signal. When you are ready to ask him to unload, tug gently on his halter and say, "Back." He may be anxious about it. Encourage him but don't try to hurry him. Let him take his time in learning the tricky business of stepping backward out of a trailer. If you excite the horse into rushing out, he may crack his head on the ceiling unless your trailer is unusually tall. Or he may lose his footing and fall.

Horses that have acquired the habit of rushing backward out of trailers can be retrained over a period of time. Each time they are unloaded, long lines must be used behind them to allow them only one step at a time. Some handlers do not bother to retrain rushers, but it is worthwhile, because such horses are dangerous not only to themselves but to bystanders.

Scramblers and Kickers

At some time or other during your ownership of horses, you may find that you have a horse that kicks or scrambles violently while inside a trailer. This problem baffles most people, and even causes some, regretfully, to sell their horses because they assume that nothing can be done about it. Yet in ninety-nine per cent of the cases the problem can be solved quite easily. The solution is so simple that no one ever believes it will work until he actually tries it.

The horse that scrambles in the trailer usually is what is known as a "climber." If you ever have a chance to observe one, you will note that he leans to one side and appears to try to "climb" the opposite wall. Unless he is removed from the trailer, he will struggle until he falls down. A horse that kicks constantly while in a trailer is not technically a climber, but his problem frequently is the same as that of the climber. *Both horses want more room to spread their feet apart so they can keep their balance, and they want that extra room on a particular side.*

The owner of a climber invariably will argue against the diagnosis. He will maintain that it is not a matter of footroom. He believes that the horse, at one time or another, received a bad scare while inside a trailer. He thinks the horse may have been stung by a bee and now has a phobia about trailers.

"He always walks right into the trailer, but once he is inside, he goes wild," the owner will say. "He may start scrambling even before the trailer moves. He never does it when he is being hauled in a van or truck."

The owner does not realize it, but he has just described a typical climber. When in a truck, a horse has all the footroom he wants.

The first question I ask such an owner, if he is seeking help, is whether he uses a double-horse trailer with a solid-walled center partition. Usually, the reply is affirmative. If so, I suggest that the partition be replaced either by a pole divider or by a divider that extends only part way to the floor. This will give the horse room to spread his feet. However, this is only part of the solution. It is necessary to know whether the horse leans to the right or to the left when he scrambles. If the horse leans to the right and scrambles with his feet against the left wall, then he should be loaded on the right side of the trailer. Without the solid center partition, he will not have anything to fight against.

If the owner says his trailer does not have a solid divider, then I ask him whether he always hauls the horse on the same side of the trailer. When the reply is affirmative, I suggest that he try the horse on the other side.

An owner who says that his horse always scrambles in a trailer, on either side of the divider partition, and who says that the divider is not solid to the floor may have that one scrambler in a hundred that is not a climber. *If his horse is a halter-puller, then that is the explanation for the problem.* A horse that fights and breaks halters when tied outside a trailer will also fight when tied inside a trailer. The solution: See to it that a rear guard chain prevents the horse from backing far enough to pull against the halter rope. Or, if the trailer aisle is narrow enough to prevent the horse from turning around, do not tie the horse's head at all.

The extra footroom is an instant cure for the climber's problem. Therefore, it is easy enough to find out whether a horse is a climber. Simply put him in a two-horse trailer without the divider and take him for a drive. If he rides quietly, the diagnosis is confirmed.

After an owner is convinced that his horse will be all right when he has room to spread his feet, he begins to worry about hauling the climber with another horse. With no solid divider, won't the climber be likely to step on the feet of the other horse? I have never known it to happen. The climber only wants an inch or so of extra space. Of course, if an owner is extremely worried about this, then his alternative is to haul the climber alone. Incidentally, the climber will travel quietly in a wide single-horse trailer, which permits him to spread his feet apart.

Horses that kick constantly while in a trailer usually can be cured of this problem as easily as climbers—by giving them more footroom. As they sometimes kick rearward instead of sideways, even though they want more room to one side, it may be necessary to experiment to learn whether they should be hauled on the right or the left side of double-horse trailers.

CHAPTER IX

First Saddling and Riding

A rider who corrals an untamed young horse, throws a saddle on his back, and then climbs aboard is asking for a bucking spree. That may prove he has nerve, but it doesn't prove he is a horseman. Even if he is a good rider, he is exposing himself and the young horse to a high risk of injury, because the horse will be frightened into a violent reaction and may lose his footing or collide with a fence. In addition, the rider takes the chance of allowing serious behavior problems to develop.

It is easy to understand why it can be frightening to a horse that is unaccustomed to human handling to be ridden for the first time. In a wild state, a horse can meet a threat from the ground, if necessary, by biting, striking, kicking, and trampling, but he is defenseless against an adversary on his back. If a beast of prey leaps on him from above, his only chance for survival is to react with sufficient violence to dislodge the animal. Small wonder that the horse will not accept a human rider calmly unless he is conditioned to trust him.

In the days when this country was young, there was a place for "buck 'em out" horsebreakers. There were men who earned a living by traveling from ranch to ranch in the West and Southwest and hiring themselves out to break colts. The colts were untamed stock, bred and foaled on the open range, and rounded up when they were old enough to be put to work. The only job of the itinerant horsebreakers was to "top them off" so that they could be turned over to ranch hands to use. Some of them became good cow ponies. Some turned out to be tricky and mean. Some didn't work out at all.

The behavior disorders that can result from rough-breaking vary from case to case. Whenever a young horse is alarmed into violence, there always is a chance that he will accidentally discover some means of disconcerting or dislodging his rider. If he does make such a discovery, the stage is set for a bad habit. The discovery may or may not involve bucking—untamed horses are not at all like rodeo broncs that can be depended upon to do nothing but jump up and down. A frightened colt may bolt, or he may rear, or whirl wildly, or even start backward and fall, before it occurs to him to try bucking. Any specific act that wins him respite is sure to be repeated in the future. Even though later attempts to use the trick are not always as successful, the horse will cling to the memory of that initial experience.

The best trainers today try to remove the risks in horse-breaking. They take time to handle colts before riding them, to allay their instinctive fears and win their confidence and respect. It is their aim, insofar as possible or for as long as possible, to avoid violent conflicts with young horses that are being started under saddle. This does not mean that they will retreat from difficulty, but that they take care not to frighten or goad young horses into a struggle.

Sooner or later, the idea of rebellion *will* occur to most young horses. The reason for making every effort to avoid inciting conflict at the outset is that the later any rebellion occurs the easier it is to quell. A horse that "acts up" during his first ride is doing so because he is frightened, and, since he cannot be expected to respond readily to controls, sometimes the best thing for the rider to do about it is nothing more than try to stay in the saddle. As the old-timers would put it, "Just stay loose and keep the horse between yourself and the ground." On the other hand, a young horse that has been ridden successfully for a week or more before he offers a tussle may not be doing it because he is afraid, but because he wants to test his rider's authority. If he has been ridden regularly and well, he will have become conditioned to a certain degree of control, and his attempts to rebel can be thwarted by decisive action on the part of a knowing rider.

Young and athletic riders sometimes are inclined to permit green horses to buck, even after controls have been established, partly because they do not know how to prevent bucking, and partly because they enjoy the admiration bestowed on them by people who think they are "marvelous riders." After all, they ask, what's the harm if a colt bucks a little now and then, so long as he doesn't win anything by throwing his rider? They don't realize that a colt that is allowed to learn that he can buck whenever he decides to do so *is* doing his share of winning against his rider, because he can and will use bucking as a trick to interrupt work. A young horse never should be allowed to discover and perfect a means of usurping his rider's control, even if it enables him to achieve dominance only for a few moments at a time. Progress in training always is slowed by lack of discipline.

When to Start Riding

How much handling and ground training should a young horse receive before he is mounted for the first time? This depends on the temperament of the horse and his response to handling, as well as on the judgment and skill of the trainer. There is much variation in the amount and nature of the handling that the top trainers of today give their young horses. Some trainers teach their colts basic ground manners, but do not longe or line-drive them. Some longe but do not line-drive, and vice versa. Others capitalize on the advantages of both longeing and line-driving.

The novice trainer is well advised to school a young horse in longeing and line-driving before starting to ride him, because, as pointed out earlier, this introduces the young horse to the discipline of work and to some of the controls that will be used in riding. He should be in no hurry to start riding, particularly if the horse is under three years of age. Most authorities agree that two-year-olds are much too immature physically to be ridden even lightly without jeopardizing their future soundness. Of course, everyone knows that many horses *are* ridden at the age of two, and sometimes are used hard, as in racing. Those that are ridden lightly *may* get by without injurious effect. Those that are ridden hard will pay for it with damage to bones, tendons, and ligaments.

Through longeing and line-driving, a young horse learns to go forward, turn, and halt in response to signals. Obviously, he does not learn to go forward in answer to *leg* signals—this he must learn after he is mounted. But he does learn to go forward on command.

The Secret of Success

Now, if you do not already know it, you are about to learn one of the great secrets of successful and sophisticated horse-breaking: If you take care not to frighten your young horse into violence during his first few rides, and *make it your primary concern from the very first to condition him to respond promptly to leg signals to go forward,* you will be able to handle almost any disciplinary problem that threatens to arise. By the time your horse reaches that stage in which it occurs to him to test your authority deliberately, perhaps by bucking or possibly by rearing, you will find that you can outwit him simply by driving him forward. It is difficult for a horse to buck forcefully, and it is impossible for him to rear, while he is moving forward. Even if your horse tests you by bolting (this can happen when he is learning to canter), you can cure him of that idea, not by making futile attempts to stop him, but by allowing him to go on and then driving him forward after he tires and wants to slow down. He will not find this test result gratifying.

The technique of using forward drive is equally valuable in countering unintentional misbehavior in a young horse. After your horse has lost his fear of being ridden, and after he is past the stage of testing your authority, he still will be green, and occasionally be startled by new experiences in his role as a saddle horse. He may jump, whirl, or shy at unusual sights and sounds. When something like this happens, you should simply drive the horse forward and resume work, as quickly and smoothly as possible. *Do not make anything of the incident by pausing either to soothe or to punish the horse,* for these are actions that tend to confirm tendencies to be skittish. Soothing and patting and cessation of work are rather pleasant rewards for "spooking." Punishment usually serves only to increase a horse's fear of an object or sound that startles him, because he remembers it in association with the aftermath of pain.

It should be emphasized here that, while the use of forward

drive forestalls many problems in the training of unspoiled horses, it will not be as helpful in working with horses that have been allowed to develop and perfect bad habits. An unspoiled horse does not know his own strength and capabilities, and so his challenges are tentative. If he understands certain controls, and they are applied in a calm but no-nonsense manner at critical moments, he will yield to them rather than risk a struggle of uncertain outcome. A spoiled horse is another story. He has succeeded in overwhelming his rider in the past, and therefore is convinced that he can do so at will. Whether his specialty is bucking, rearing, whirling, shying, or bolting, he has become an expert at violence and is unlikely to respond to any normal controls that are intended to thwart misbehavior. Before he can be expected to give up his bad habit, he must somehow be taught that it is unrewarding. In some cases, particularly in young horses that have only recently learned their bad habits, the problems can be overcome by clever tactics and skillful riding; in other cases, outright punishment is necessary. When punishment is inflicted, it must be appropriate and precisely timed, or it is worse than useless.

If you are an inexperienced trainer, and you have a horse that has developed a dangerously bad habit, you should seek the personal assistance of an expert without delay. The handling and retraining of problem horses requires knowledge, confidence, and skill. To some extent, knowledge can be acquired from conversation and reading, but the ability to react confidently and skillfully in perilous situations comes only with practice. There is little or no margin for error in working with a badly spoiled horse—every time you fail to cope with his misbehavior, his habit is reinforced.

How can you find a trainer who is qualified to help you with a *problem* horse? By looking for someone who is experienced and expert at starting *unspoiled* young horses under saddle. A trainer who has worked extensively with young horses knows where problems originate, and knows what it takes to overcome them. More than that, he knows how to substitute good habits for bad habits *while he is overcoming the bad habits*. Unless this is done, a problem horse will remain a problem—he may seem to be cured of a bad habit, but the defiant attitude will be unchanged. He may become the kind of horse that always tests his riders, and takes advantage of them when they show weakness.

It is to be hoped that your young horse does not have any dangerously bad habits. Of course, if he has never been ridden at all, he has *no* habits under saddle, either good or bad, and it is up to you to see to it that he gets started right. If you have taught the horse good manners and obedience in longeing and line-driving, you already have demonstrated that you have something of what it takes to be a trainer and a horseman, and you are ready to move on.

Even with an unspoiled young horse, you will have difficulties because you will be learning as you train. You are certain to make mistakes, as all people (and all horses) do when they are learning. In fact, no matter how expert you become as a trainer in the future, you will make mistakes. The difference between the novice and the expert is that the latter makes fewer mistakes and they are less apparent. The advantage in working with an unspoiled horse is that there is a margin for error. If a problem arises and you do not handle it correctly, it does not necessarily follow that the horse will develop a bad habit from that single experience. You should profit from the experience, however, by giving thought to it and deciding what to do about the problem the next time it occurs. If it develops that you cannot handle the problem, and there are indications that the horse is beginning to realize it and take advantage of it, don't hesitate to seek qualified assistance.

Before you mount your young horse for the first time, familiarize him with the equipment that you will be using when riding. One of the best ways to accustom a horse to a saddle is to longe him with it on his back for several consecutive days, until he accepts it without the slightest anxiety. If you are going to use a bridle with a bit, line-drive him with a snaffle for several days. If you are going to ride with a bosal, line-drive him with a bosal.

Choosing a Saddle

The type of saddle that you use when breaking a horse in to riding is unimportant, insofar as the horse is concerned, so feel free to use any kind of saddle you like. Some people seem to think that a stock saddle gives a young horse the notion that he is destined to be a cow pony, and that a flat saddle inclines him to be a jumper or a gaited horse. Nothing of the sort. It is the rider and not the saddle that trains a horse, and it is only when a horse is ready to enter specialized schooling that the saddle makes a difference. Even then, the difference is less significant to the horse than to the rider. Saddles are constructed in various styles for practical reasons, primarily to make it easy for riders to adopt various positions or "seats" that are appropriate to the type of work their horses perform. A stock saddle, while well suited to pleasure riding or cattle work, is worse than no saddle at all for jumping. A jumping saddle, with forward flaps designed to accommodate the bent knees of riders, is totally unsatisfactory for working with dressage or saddle show horses in fully collected gaits.

A stock saddle does offer greater security than a flat saddle in moments of unexpected violence. The higher shoulders and cantle can prevent a rider from lurching too far forward or backward, and the relatively inflexible stirrup leathers make it easier for the rider to recover a stirrup if a foot slips out. The greatest disadvantage of a stock saddle is that the horn can be dangerous in a fall. (Rodeo bronc saddles have no horns, because contestants have been fatally injured by them.)

If you routinely ride a flat saddle, and either do not have or do not like a stock saddle, there is no reason for you to make a change. After all, you are not rough-breaking a colt. The care that you have taken in preparing your young horse for the experience of being ridden is better security against mishaps than any saddle of any design.

Techniques in Saddling

Whatever the saddle that you decide to use, introduce it to your horse with an easy and reassuring manner, so that he will develop no problems about being saddled. Poor technique in saddling can cause a variety of bad habits. Some young horses, because of careless trainers, become saddle-shy and this is a trait that is difficult to overcome. No matter how expertly they are handled in later years, they may always cringe or grow tense with alarm when a saddle is lifted toward them. Some horses, although not taught to be afraid of saddling, are allowed to develop a habit of fidgeting restlessly during the process. Many learn to "puff up" whenever their girths are tightened. The worst problem is yet to be named: Some horses, in the hands of poor trainers, become "cinch-bound." It is their curious habit to throw themselves or sink to the ground whenever their girths are suddenly drawn tight.

For the benefit of readers who have never heard of cinch-bound horses, more detail is in order. Anyone who handles horses should be able to recognize the slightest signs of the vice; otherwise, he might someday unknowingly buy trouble. Only recently, two women asked me to accompany them to a horse dealer's barn to give them my opinion of a hunter prospect. The women stood by while the dealer saddled the horse, but they did not appear to notice what happened when the dealer drew the girth tight. The instant the girth was tightened, there was a sharp catch in the horse's breath and the animal seemed to be immobilized. Then he started to sink backward. With flying fingers the dealer loosened the girth, just in time to save the situation. The horse relaxed and straightened up. Without saying a word, the dealer led the horse forward a few steps, then carefully drew the girth a little tighter. Then he led the horse a few more steps. Then he tightened the girth a little more. Still, the women seemed to notice nothing of interest. Finally, the dealer succeeded in securing the saddle. As it turned out, the horse showed a lameness which the dealer could not explain, and the women decided on that basis that they did not want the horse. Later I told them it was all for the best, because the horse was cinch-bound, in addition to being lame.

As indicated by the incident related above, it is possible to work around the vice of some cinch-bound horses by using a bit of sleight-of-hand in securing their saddles. It is a risk to buy such horses, however, particularly from a dealer who acquires much of his stock from auction barns. All too often, incurable vices are the reason horses are sold through auctions. In extreme cases, cinch-bound horses reach a stage in which they simply will not tolerate a tightened girth, no matter how slowly and carefully it is drawn. They will go down and refuse to get up until the girth is loosened. Is there any way to overcome the problem? I know of instances in which *temporary* cures have been effected, usually by shock treatments such as harmless but frightening whackings with kitchen brooms, administered after the horses have thrown themselves down. As part of the treatment, the horses are *held* down for the punishment. The object is to convince them that it is best for them to stay on their feet. Sometimes this treatment seems to work, but I have never known a case in which the results were lasting. Perhaps this is because the horses were handled inexpertly thereafter. Cinch-bound horses are closely akin to balky horses, in that their tactic is passive resistance, and any "cures" endure only so long as the follow-up handling is subtle and skillful.

There is no need for your young horse to develop *any* problems about being saddled. It is easy to develop a good technique in saddling—the only reason that more people don't have it is that they never give it any thought.

If you are planning to use an older saddle in the early riding of your horse, examine it carefully to be sure that it will be comfortable to the horse, and is sturdy enough to stand rough riding if necessary. The tree should fit well, and it goes without saying that it should not be cracked or broken. If the saddle is a stock saddle, the girth should be soft, wide, and clean. If it is a flat saddle, the girth should be flexible and clean. A dirty girth is an irritant, especially to skin that has not been toughened to the wearing of a girth. On a stock saddle, check the cinch latigos, and the leather thongs or metal fasteners that secure the stirrup leathers. They may be worn and need replacement. On a flat saddle, assure yourself that the billet straps and stirrup leathers are in good condition. Of course, if you are buying a new saddle for the horse, you can choose one that is comfortable and safe.

Before putting the saddle on the horse's back for the first time, you can prepare him for the feeling of a girth by longeing him with a surcingle. If you don't have a surcingle, it will be worth your while to borrow one. Put it on him, and draw it just snug enough to hold it in place. Longe him with it, then draw it a little tighter, and longe him again.

When tightening a surcingle or girth of any kind, it is extremely important to do it swiftly and smoothly. People who jerk and snatch and fuss with girths, spending several minutes on a task that should require only seconds, invariably make their horses peevish about it. And the longer they take to adjust the girths, the more time they give their horses to figure out ways of making trouble. Most commonly, horses that are saddled clumsily learn to "puff up" aginst the tightening of their girths.

It is also important *not* to draw a girth suddenly and severely tight on a young horse. *This is what causes horses to become cinch-bound.*

After your horse has been longed with the surcingle, remove it, and then spend a few minutes acquainting him with the saddle blanket or pad. Rub him with the pad, and rustle it over his back. Put it on him and take it off several times. Because of his early sacking and other handling, he should have no fear of it. However, if he is anxious, work with him until he is calm, using the sacking technique.

Even though you expect your horse to accept the saddle calmly, have a friend hold him the first time you put it on his back. Don't try to hold the halter rope yourself while you work. If anything does startle the colt, you will need both hands free to handle the saddle. Allowing a saddle to slip and fall off a colt when he moves suddenly is one way to make him saddle-shy.

When you lift the saddle onto the horse, do it with an easy and confident manner. Most people who have poor technique in saddling young horses are either too cautious and gingerly about it or too rough. A timid approach makes a colt uneasy. Roughness frightens him.

If you are using a stock saddle, and you know how to swing it onto his back in one gliding motion, do so, but take care not to allow the saddle to jar the horse, and hold the girth so that he will not be struck by a flying cinch buckle. If you cannot handle a stock saddle this way, and must push it upward to place it on the horse's back, then fold the off-side (right) stirrup back over the seat before you lift the saddle. Once the saddle is on the horse's back, lower the stirrup to its proper place.

If you have a flat saddle, run the stirrups up the leathers before you put the saddle on the horse, and leave them there. Always leave the stirrups up on a flat saddle until you are ready to ride. When they are dangling free, they can strike and bruise a horse's elbows. Also, they can be caught against fixed objects.

After you have placed the saddle on the horse's back, leave it there for a few moments, keeping your hands on it so that you can prevent it from falling off. Rock and jostle it a little to show the horse that it is harmless, then take it off. As you did with the saddle pad, put it on and take it off several times, giving the horse a brief rest between times. Remember that when you are introducing something new to a horse, he worries about the possibility that you are building up to something that will hurt him. By repetitively putting the saddle on and taking it off, you are reassuring him that nothing dangerous is going to happen. Do this whether the horse seems worried or not, just to be on the safe side.

The next step is to put the saddle on and secure the girth. The horse should not object to this if you have given him a workout on the longe line with a surcingle, and if you are careful not to draw the girth too tight. The girth *must* be drawn tight enough to hold the saddle in place, but it should not be as tight as you would fasten it for riding.

When tightening the girth, don't dawdle. There always is a possibility that even the best-prepared young horse will react with a sudden start when he realizes that the saddle is being pinned to his back. If he acts up before the girth is fully secured, he may be in for a terrifying experience. The saddle might slip underneath him. If it does, he will struggle and kick in panic until the saddle breaks free, or until he is rendered helpless by injury or exhaustion.

As soon as you have secured the girth, take the halter shank in hand. Then exchange the halter shank for a longe line, and lead the colt. If the colt becomes frightened while being led, it is easier and safer to control him with a longe line. Don't let him get away; however, if he wants to buck, pay out the line and let him buck. Let him find out that he cannot rid himself of the saddle. Then lead him again. Take a long, sauntering walk if he is hot and needs cooling. Do not pause to allow him to graze. He might forget for a moment that he is wearing a saddle, and then, upon moving, be frightened.

Before returning him to his stall or pasture for the day, give him a light longeing session with the saddle. Again, if he wants to buck, allow him to buck, but put him back to work as soon as he ceases. You might draw the girth a little tighter before concluding the workout. You will find that it doesn't bother him.

For two or three days, longe him with the saddle. If he shows any tendency to become fidgety about saddling, review your technique. Be certain you are doing nothing the horse finds unpleasant. Also, make it a practice to tie the horse for saddling. This is an effective aid in teaching him to stand still.

Bits and Bitting

Now the subject of bitting arises. Are you going to start riding your horse with a bit, or do you plan to start with a bosal and graduate to the bit in a later stage of training? If you are going to use a bit at the outset, should it be a snaffle or a curb?

There probably are more debates about bitting than any other subject in the training of horses. This would seem to indicate that bitting is a complicated matter, but it is not, or at least it should not be, to anyone who fully understands what he is trying to do with his horse at a given level of training.

The primary goal in the basic training of a young horse under saddle is simply to teach the horse to carry a rider and to respond obediently and calmly to signals to move at various gaits. At this stage, the only purpose of any headgear on the horse, whether bridle or hackamore, is to provide the rider with a means of turning, slowing, and halting the horse. Therefore, it can be very simple, and although it must afford adequate control, *it should be something that the rider is capable of using without making the horse fearful or defiant.*

In more advanced schooling, the ultimate goal will be to teach the horse to perform at his athletic best in a selected specialty. In most cases, this means that the trainer will want to "educate the mouth" of the horse. A horse's mouth is said to be educated when the horse understands and complies with signals to collect (gather) himself and shorten or extend his stride. Thus, in advanced schooling, the headgear is used for more than merely turning and stopping the horse—it also serves as a means of regulating the horse's posture and length of stride. It must be a bridle with bitting that permits subtlety of control.

What does this mean to you? It means that during basic training you can ride your young horse with any kind of headgear that you think will serve you best as a means of turning, slowing, and stopping the horse. It means that you can use a bridle with a snaffle, or a bridle with a curb or Pelham bit, or a hackamore with bosal. The only proviso is that your choice should be based on an objective self-appraisal of your abilities and on an understanding of the advantages and disadvantages of the various bitting practices. (If, after reading this chapter, you find it difficult to make a decision, it might be well for you to start with something that is used by the top horsemen in your area, so that you can go to them for advice when necessary.)

If you are an avid reader of books on horsemanship, then you may be surprised at this treatment of the subject of bitting. As you know, some authorities recommend starting young horses in the snaffle and *only* the snaffle. Some recommend the bosal. Very few recommend the curb or Pelham, even though they are widely used.

Forget about books for a moment, and take a look at the real world. Have you ever enjoyed the privilege of watching a fine trainer at work with a young horse? Did you judge the trainer by the equipment he used or by the results he achieved? Wouldn't it be ridiculous to condemn a trainer for putting curb bits in the mouths of young horses if he consistently turned out cheerful and willing performers?

In talking to expert horsemen, including those who write books, you will find few who will criticize other experts for their bitting practices. As someone once said, "Among great horsemen, bitting is a small subject." This is because the experts know that bits and bosals are not in themselves "keys" to success in training, as so many novices wishfully believe. It is how they are used that is important.

Why is it, then, that the experts express strong prejudices for and against various bitting practices when they write books (or teach clinics)? It is because they are concerned with the fact that in their books (and clinics) they usually are addressing less-than-expert riders, and they want to recommend practices that they feel are most suitable for general application. To put it plainly, they know that most riders have "pulling hands," and that pulling hands cause problems with *all* bits. The *types* of problems that occur depend, to a great extent, on the *types* of bits that the riders use. Some problems are worse than others in that they are more dangerous or more difficult to overcome. Therefore, the experts want to recommend bitting practices that they believe are least likely to result in serious trouble if misused. They usually have strong opinions on this subject.

Here is a brief discussion of bits and bosals and the types of problems they engender when used by riders with pulling hands:

Snaffle—The jointed snaffle, which is the most commonly used snaffle, has a "nutcracker" action in the mouth of the horse. If it is used by a rider with pulling hands, the horse soon learns that he can reduce the discomfort of the pinching by "poking his nose out." When a horse travels with his nose extended forward, he hollows his back, and this causes him to move awkwardly. If the jointed snaffle is used severely enough to make the horse afraid of the bit, the horse also becomes high-headed, and develops a tendency to withdraw the head toward the rider in response to a pull on the reins. Some experts recommend that the jointed snaffle be used in combination with a running martingale, so that the reins are kept low and the horse cannot evade the action of the bit by raising his head. However, unless the rider learns to control the horse without pulling, the running martingale will not "cure" the horse of his problems. The half-moon snaffle is milder than the jointed snaffle, because it has no pinching action, but it is not commonly used, even by experts. Most riders find that it is *too* mild. As one expert expressed it, "A bit must have *some* authority, else it is useless in emergencies."

Curb—The curb bit operates on a leverage principle, and so it multiplies the force of any action exerted by the rider. The leverage ratio is determined by the length of the shanks and the tightness of the curb strap. In effect, it puts the horse's lower jaw in a vise. Obviously, the curb can be a severe bit in pulling hands. The spade bit, which has an extremely high port, is a variety of curb bit that can be even more severe because it produces action against the roof of the mouth. (Even the experts who use spade bits do not use them on green horses. They start their colts in hackamores.) When curb bits are misused, many horses quickly discover that they can find some relief from the leverage action by bowing (overflexing) their necks. Overflexed horses have a tendency to be overbalanced forward, which makes it difficult for them to turn or reduce pace readily, and so they become "pullers," in self-defense against pulling hands. Horses that do not discover the trick of overflexion may become anxious head-tossers, or they may, like horses mistreated by the snaffle, become high-headed and draw their heads back when the reins are used. The latter reaction to a curb bit is extremely undesirable in a young horse. Because it gives him little relief from the leverage of the bit, the horse may next try rearing, and rearing may get to be a habit.

Curb with jointed mouthpiece—Novices often use this when training young horses because they think it is a mild version of the curb bit. They are wrong. It is a severe bit, combining the nutcracker action of the snaffle with the leverage action of the curb.

Pelham—This bit also offers both snaffle and curb actions, but it is not at all like the curb with the jointed mouthpiece. The Pelham, which does not have a jointed mouthpiece, is supposed to serve as "two bits in one," and has rings for two pairs of reins. The rider can use one pair of reins for a snaffle effect, and the other pair of reins for curb action. However, riders who have pulling hands are rarely capable of using the reins discriminately. Unless they leave one pair of reins completely slack, they invariably pull on both pairs simultaneously. In a sense, this is an advantage to the horse, for the pulling on the snaffle reins does, to some extent, negate the leverage of the curb. Therefore, by default, the Pelham is a milder bit than the plain curb.

Hackamore—There are two general types of hackamores, both "bitless bridles" designed to exert pressure across the nose and under the jaw of a horse. One type is the hackamore with the rawhide bosal, which loosely encircles the horse's nose. It usually is preferred by hackamore experts, especially for starting young horses. The other type is a hackamore with a noseband, curb strap or curb chain, and bit-like shanks. It sometimes is called a "beartrap" or "mechanical" hackamore. It is popularly used by Western riders whose horses are "bit-shy." It is not considered suitable for horses unless they are responsive to neck-reining, because pulling on the reins separately twists the shanks into awkward positions. The bosal that is used in starting the training of young horses is stiff and heavy. It must be carefully adjusted to fit a horse, and must be used skillfully. A rider who has pulling hands can get into serious trouble with a bosal; the usual result is a bull-headed horse. Whenever you hear anyone say, "I've tried bosals but they are no good, because horses run right through them," you are listening to a heavy-handed rider.

This brief description of problems that are brought about by the *misuse* of various bitting practices is not intended to be discouraging, but to help you decide which type of bridle you are going to use in the basic training of your young horse. If you know that you do not have pulling hands, then you can confidently use anything you please. If you either know or suspect that you have pulling hands (because in your riding experience you have encountered some of the problems mentioned above), then you should choose a type of bitting least likely to lead to serious problems. As stated earlier, most authorities recommend the snaffle. In comparison with the curb bit, it is relatively mild, unless it is used very crudely, because force used by a rider is not multiplied by leverage. Of course, no one wants a horse to develop a habit of "poking his nose out" and moving with a sprawling gait, but if this problem does appear when a snaffle is used, and the rider recognizes it early, it is easier to correct than overflexion. A horse that overflexes and gets "behind the bit" is fearful of contact with the bit, and it can be extremely difficult to erase that fear and teach him to accept a rider's hands.

Whatever you decide to use, this book is written on the assumption that the general reader is a less-than-expert rider, and one of its purposes is to help the reader learn to control his horse without pulling. The foundation already has been laid, in the earlier discussions of the use of the fixed hand (instead of the pulling hand), in overcoming any resistances of a horse when it is being led, longed, or driven in long lines.

You may be curious about the advisability of using unconventional bitting practices in the training of young horses. If you have difficulty with a colt, should you try items such as twisted wire snaffles, gag bits, draw reins, etc.? Not if it is your ambition to become an accomplished horseman. In training a young horse, you have a great opportunity to develop good hands, and you can depend on the horse to let you know how you are progressing. If the horse begins to develop problems, try to find out what it is that *you* are doing wrong, and try to do something about it. Don't go shopping for mechanical gimmicks—they will not solve *your* problems, and they may have an adverse effect on the horse. Mechanical gimmicks sometimes are helpful in the management and control of spoiled horses, but they have no place in the intelligent basic training of young horses.

What about changing from one conventional bit to another? If you start a colt in a snaffle, and encounter difficulty, is it all right to change to a curb bit or Pelham? This may be a good idea. Let's say, for instance, that you are working your young horse in a snaffle, and are fairly well satisfied with his progress, but despite your best efforts to use your hands correctly the horse begins to point his nose forward. You know that if he is allowed to do this very long it will affect his way of going. If you feel certain that you cannot handle the problem, and there is no one to help you through it, then you might try a bit with curb action. This will buy a little time. In a bit with curb action, the horse will discover that there is no reward in raising his nose, and it may be a while before it occurs to him to try the opposite tactic of overflexion. In the meantime, you can be giving more thought to the continuing improvement of the use of your hands.

Nothing has been said of the full bridle or so-called double bridle, which has both the snaffle and curb bits. Certainly, this is a conventional bridle, but it is seldom used in basic training. It could be used, but the snaffle that normally accompanies the full bridle is smaller in diameter, and thus can be rather severe. A snaffle for a young horse should be large, curved, and smooth. Such a snaffle together with a curb bit would be a bulky and unnecessary mouthful for a young horse. Full bridles usually are reserved for the final stages of training of horses that are ridden and shown in fully collected gaits, such as saddle show horses and dressage horses. Expert horsemen employ them with great subtlety to regulate posture and control flexion.

If you want to give your young horse the best possible preparation for future "mouth education," then do not attempt to shape his posture during basic training. Make every effort to avoid causing *faulty* carriage, but do not try to collect the horse. Schooling for collection should come only after a horse has learned to carry a rider calmly and obediently and in good balance.

As pointed out in Chapter II, there are trainers who start teaching their horses collection from the beginning of their work under saddle. More accurately, it should be said that they start *conditioning* their horses to adopt an attitude of collection *automatically* whenever they are mounted and ridden. Many saddle show horse trainers routinely teach their horses collection by "spooking" them, because horses naturally gather themselves for action when they are excited. Horses look beautiful when they are fully collected, with their necks arched and their tails high, and in saddle show horse classes they are required to work in full collection. However, horses that are conditioned into collection by the anxiety method are not useful for anything but their specialties. They do not have "educated mouths" in the sense that they understand and respond to signals to increase and decrease their degree of collection, and to shorten or lengthen stride. Why do trainers use shortcut methods to teach their horses collection? They do it to save time. Beyond that, many do it because it is the only way they know how to do it. Hopefully, if and when you decide to learn to school your horse in collection, you will not look for shortcuts, but will study and follow the classic principles of horsemanship. Just as horses can be "broken to ride" without force or fear, they can be taught collection without force or fear.

Once you have decided on the bridle that you will use at the outset of your young horse's training, see to it that both the headstall and the bit or bosal fit comfortably and well. The mouthpiece of a bit should be just wide enough to lie comfortably in the horse's mouth without slipping from side to side when the reins are used. A new bosal will have to be soaked in water and shaped so that it does not pinch against the sides of the horse's jaws when the reins are inactive. Find a way to brace it for drying, and it will hold the desired contours.

When adjusting a hackamore on a horse, be certain that the bosal lies above the soft cartilage of the nose. Otherwise, just how high or low it should be depends upon the individual horse. Experiment to find out where your horse "likes it best."

If you are going to use a bridle in preference to a hackamore, introduce the horse to the feeling of a bit in his mouth in two stages:

1. Simply let the horse wear a bridle *with a snaffle* for an hour or so daily for several days, both in a stall and while being longed. Do not attach any reins to the snaffle, and do not attach a longe line to the snaffle. Any leading or longeing should be done by means of a halter or cavesson placed over or under the headstall of the bridle. At first, the colt will be mystified by the presence of the bit in his mouth. He will chew on it, and try to work it out of his mouth. Within a few days, he will cease to worry about it. (Ignore the advice of any well-meaning friends who suggest putting the colt in a bitting harness to teach him to "give" to the bit or to "set his head." A bitting harness used for such purposes is nothing more than a gimmick, and it may instill a habit of overflexion. When experts use a bitting harness, they use it solely as an aid in schooling for collection.)

2. After the colt has become accustomed to the sensation of the snaffle in his mouth, line-drive him from the ground with the snaffle. *A horse should never be line-driven with a curb bit,* even though the trainer may plan to ride him with one. The curb bit is extremely severe in driving lines, and is almost certain to cause overflexion. A young horse that has been carefully and successfully introduced to driving with a cavesson or halter will make the transition to driving in a snaffle with little difficulty. All work should be at the walk, and, during the first few driving sessions, the turns and halts should be very gradual. Always forewarn the horse of a halt by using voice commands *before* using the lines. The objective is to induce him to halt voluntarily in response to a light signal from the lines. Do not try to *pull* him to a halt. Use *resisting* hands. When you are ready to stop, simply establish a "feel" of his mouth, then set your hands and stop walking. The first time you try to stop the horse with the bit, he may be somewhat frightened by the new sensation, and it may not occur to him that he is supposed to stop. If so, don't fight him. Relax the lines and let him go on a few steps, then repeat the voice command and the signal. It may be necessary to do this several times, but after a while the horse will realize there is nothing to fear and he will be able to pay attention to your signals. If your horse starts developing a habit of opening his mouth widely before he halts, it means that you are unconsciously pulling him to a halt, instead of

waiting for him to halt for you. Be careful—this is a critical time in bitting, and a critical time in the education of your hands. The horse should learn to respond to the lines without opening his mouth and without bowing his neck. If all goes well, he will learn to reduce pace as soon as he feels resistance. *After* the horse has learned to respond correctly to the bit, he may once or twice test the lines by deliberately refusing to reduce pace. You will know that he is trying an experiment because he will show no signs of fear. When that happens, fix your hands and do *not* yield. He may pull hard, and his mouth may open, but he will give up and no bad habit will result. As you will remember from your earlier work, it is normal for a horse to make "one last try" before he surrenders completely to a new kind of control. When turning the horse, use the same technique of resisting instead of pulling. Establish a "feel" of the bit with one hand, then set it, and yield with the other hand as the horse starts turning. If the horse starts developing a habit of "rubbernecking" (overbending the neck sideways before and during turning), then you will know you are using pulling hands. Again, be careful. Make the turns *gradual* until the horse gets the right idea.

When line-driving a horse with a bosal, attach the lines to the heel knot. The curb action of the bosal is not as strong when line-driving as when riding, because the hands are in a lower position; therefore, the signals that you give for slowing and halting the horse will be felt primarily across the nose. To the horse, the hackamore will seem much like a halter, except that the nosepiece will be heavier and more solid.

There is one important difference between the techniques of driving with a bosal and driving with a bit. When the horse decides to test the authority of the bosal by pulling against your hands, you may not be able to hold him simply by standing and resisting. In a pulling bout, the bosal is not as severe as the bit. If the horse does start pulling against you, *lighten the lines* so that the bosal will be loose and you can "bump" his nose with a sharp and meaningful jerk on one of the lines. You *must* show him that you can make the bosal unpleasant, else you will lose control.

The more line-driving you do, whether with a bit or a bosal, the better your young horse will be prepared for control while riding.

Technique in Bridling

Are you skillful at putting a bridle on a horse? It is just as important to do this well as it is to handle a saddle deftly. Perhaps you have seen horses that resist bridling, either by raising their heads high, or by refusing to open their mouths for the bit, or by jerking away when the leather touches their ears. They have developed these bad habits because they have been handled crudely. If they are violent in their resistances, it is because they have been handled crudely and then punished for their defensive misbehavior.

In putting a bridle on your young horse for the first time, be prepared to be patient and gentle. Of course, your colt is accustomed to having his head handled, because he has worn halters, and so there is no reason why he should raise his head high or be fretful about his ears. The only thing that will be new to him is the bit. Do not try to make him open his mouth for the bit by bumping it against his teeth. Simply insert your thumb in the corner of his mouth and rub or press downward on the bar of the jaw. As soon as the mouth opens, slip the bit into place, then quickly and smoothly adjust the headstall. If you are slow and clumsy about putting the crownpiece over and behind the ears, the bit may dangle loosely and rattle against the teeth. This is not necessarily painful to a horse, but it can make him nervous. In cold weather, it is a good idea to warm the bit in your hands.

Eventually, you will want your horse to learn to "take the bit" without waiting for you to insert your thumb in his mouth. After he has become accustomed to the bridle and bit, start making it a practice to hold the bit gently against the juncture of his front teeth for a few seconds before using your thumb to open his mouth. Soon, he will start opening his mouth voluntarily.

Be as thoughtful about removing the bridle as you are about putting it on the horse. Slip the crownpiece smoothly over his ears, and then wait for the horse to relax his mouth and work the bit out with a gentle chewing action. Pulling the bit out roughly

First mounting of a young Saddlebred Bob Black eases onto the back of a young horse while Tim Roberts holds him and speaks soothingly. It is apparent that the horse's balance is unsteady, because he has not yet learned to brace himself against weight in one stirrup. The ears are in a "neutral" position, neither pinned back in anger nor inattentive to the rider.

Relaxing and accepting the weight of a rider, the young horse is stroked reassuringly. As this is the first time the horse has been mounted, the trainer may not ask him to step forward. He may only mount and dismount several times, then unsaddle him and return him to his stall, giving him time to absorb the lesson.

Following a well-trained older horse on a cross-country ride, a young horse calmly negotiate obstacles that might otherwise be upsetting. Cross-country excursions are a pleasant way t accustom a young horse to carrying a rider. Work in a confined area, such as an arena or sma pasture, can quickly become boring and result in a sour attitude. Shown here is Jeff Forbes o his pinto, Little Man, followed by Cindy Berke on Holly.

Downhill at a walk Young horses should not be allowed to rush downhill or uphill. Going downhill puts a lot of stress on the forelegs, especially when a horse is green and awkward. Cantering or bounding uphill is very hard on the hind legs. Tina Brown and her Quarter Horse gelding, Ole Gold Bar.

Riding with a bosal instead of a bit during early training may be advisable if a horse is unduly fretful about a bit. After the horse has learned to move calmly and obediently at all gaits, the bit can be introduced without trauma. It is important, however, that the rider learn to use the bosal correctly before trying it on a young horse. Dino Gerard and her young Thoroughbred gelding, Huck.

Cantering on a light rein In early training, the horse should be encouraged to relax into stead
paces on a light rein. When the horse can maintain an easy canter without "spilling forward," i
means he is finding a good state of balance under a rider. It also means he is developin
confidence in his rider. Colonel Alfred R. Kitts and his Thoroughbred gelding, Coppe
Challenge.

Dismounting at the barn gate as a routine practice after riding can cause a horse to be "barn-bound." The trainer of a young horse should be especially careful to choose a different place every day to quit work. Otherwise, whenever the horse becomes tired or annoyed, it will want to head for the spot where the rider usually gets off. Wendy Bletz and her Anglo-Arab gelding, Shane.

...ustration will be the result of allowing a horse ... graze while being ridden. Soon the horse ...gins to insist on grazing, despite protests from ... rider. Dino Gerard and pony hunter, Irish ...st.

People can be pushovers At one time or another, it will occur to a horse to try using his handler as a "scratching post." Unless the attempt is quickly discouraged, head-rubbing will become a nuisance. Joan Baird and Moki.

Raising his nose high enables a horse to evade the full effect of the snaffle bit. When the horse's head is in this position, pressure of the bit is felt more in the soft corners of the mouth than on the unyielding bars of the jaw. It is a common defense against pain caused by pulling hands. A young horse that is ridden in a snaffle bit will start doing this if the rider "hangs on his mouth" or tries to make him turn or stop too quickly for his level of training.

Confidence in the rider's hands If a young horse is unafraid of the snaffle bit, he will travel with his head in a normal position, as shown here. He will willingly accept the action of the bit against the bars of the jaw, because, under a tactful rider, he learns that if he yields to pressure the pressure disappears. Pearl O'Connell and her four-year-old Thoroughbred gelding, Joe Casey.

Rubbernecking into a turn Pulling a horse's head around to make him turn will result in a clumsy maneuver. The rider's objective should be to ride the horse through turns with the neck only slightly bent.

ell-balanced for a turn With his neck nt in the direction of movement, the rse steps smartly into a sharp right rn. He is responding to a slight pres- re (not a hard pull) on the right rein. tty Howell and Cassell's Abantis.

Learning the rein-back When a horse steps backward, his legs should move in diagonal pairs. Only then can the movement be balanced and straight. This horse is learning to rein back but has not yet achieved perfection. The legs on the ground—the cannon bones—should be in alignment. Colonel Alfred R. Kitts during the early training of Copper Challenge.

and jarring it against the horse's teeth will cause him to develop a habit of throwing his head back when he is unbridled.

There is one unmannerly trick that novices often indulgently allow their horses to learn. If you want your horse to be well trained about the removal of his bridle, don't let him help you take it off. He should keep his head still while you unfasten the throatlatch and when you reach for the crownpiece. Sooner or later, it will occur to him to try to hurry you. He will tilt his head toward you and fidget impatiently while you work with the throatlatch. When you grasp the crownpiece, he will try to twist his head out of the bridle. If he is allowed to do this, he may become so "helpful" that he makes it difficult for you to remove the bridle, and may even cause you to hurt his mouth. This problem is like all other problems—it is easier to prevent than to overcome. All you have to do is make it plain to him that you will do it your way or not at all. If you start to remove the bridle, and he starts fidgeting, then *pause and wait.* Resume work only when his head becomes still. That's all there is to it.

First Mounting

In view of all the preparation you have made, the first mounting of your horse should be a quiet experience. Choose a nice day for it, whether you are going indoors or outdoors. Strong winds are distracting to horses. Extremely cold weather invigorates them. Choose a day when nothing unusual is happening at your stable. This is no time to have your colt on edge because carpenters are hammering on a roof.

First, saddle and bridle your horse and give him a settling workout on the longe line. At the conclusion of the session, ask a friend to hold the horse while you mount. Explain to your friend that you are going to be slow and casual about it, and ask him not to grip the horse tightly. He will serve as a steadying influence, because the horse is accustomed to being controlled from the ground. He should not hold the horse by the reins, but by a lead line or a longe line.

Check the girth for security, then start acquainting the horse with the feeling of weight in the left stirrup by pressing down on it with the heel of one hand. If this does not bother him, place the toe of your foot in the stirrup and press down. Then remove your foot from the stirrup and find something to do for a minute or so. You might brush the horse's neck, or clean a hoof. After the interruption, replace your toe in the stirrup and spring gently up and down a few times, just high enough to allow the stirrup to catch a little weight. Then give the horse another brief rest. Repeat this several times. This is another application of the psychology you used in sacking the horse. The little rest periods reassure the horse that your intentions are harmless, and his tolerance grows.

When the horse shows no concern about your springing in the stirrup, go a little further. Facing the saddle, and taking great care not to dig your toe into his side, step upward smoothly and easily and lean your weight across the saddle. Keep your upper body bent low over the horse. Do not straddle the horse, and do not straighten up. Be ready to kick your toe out of the stirrup and slide down if anything goes wrong, because you are in no position to try to stay on his back. Nothing should go wrong if you have stepped up smoothly and easily. (If you feel you are not able to do this athletically, then ask another friend to help by giving you a "leg up.") Don't stay on the horse more than half a minute or so. Before anything *does* go wrong, give him a pat and slip off, and then give him another rest.

If the horse has been unusually nervous about all this, then he has had enough for the day. Let him sleep on it, and he will be calmer the second day. Chances are, however, that your horse will not be unusually nervous. In the training that has gone beforehand, he has developed confidence in you.

When the horse seems to accept your weight across the saddle without fear, then mount him astride, keeping your upper body bent low. After you are in the saddle, straighten up very gradually, patting the horse and talking to him. Confidence or no confidence, he will be startled instinctively when you tower over him. Sit easily and do not grip with your legs. After a few moments, bend forward again and quietly dismount.

For three or four days, practice mounting and dismounting. Always longe the horse first, to eliminate any surplus of energy.

Have someone standing by to hold him while you mount and dismount. Stay in the saddle for several minutes at a time. If you have no one to hold the horse, tie him, or, if you feel there will be no problems, take up the reins, and start using them as necessary to prevent the horse from moving out of place.

As the horse becomes accustomed to the mounting and dismounting, start being deliberately "careless." Don't be too rough at first, but allow your leg to brush across his hindquarters when you mount, rock around in the saddle, and lean down to dust a speck off one boot and then the other. Reach forward and scratch his ears, and rub your legs on his sides. Practice mounting and dismounting from the right side. In short, do everything a heedless child might do. A horse should learn not to be timid about unexpected gestures.

First Riding

After this is done, the horse is ready for riding. The sensation of carrying a living burden is going to feel strange to him, and it will feel different to him at each of his gaits. In addition, he will be a little excited by the faster gaits. Therefore, he should be allowed to become accustomed to carrying a rider at a walk before he is asked to trot, and at a trot before he is asked to canter. Plan on riding him at least a week before graduation to a trot.

Start your riding in a small enclosure or on a longe line, so that the horse will not be tempted to try a brisk gallop before control is established. The fact that he responds to the bit or bosal while line-driving gives you a decided head start on handling him from the saddle, but things *are* different now, because your presence on his back while he is moving makes him uneasy. And *you* may be a little different now. You may not feel quite as sure of yourself as you did when you were on the ground. If you are a little edgy, try not to let it affect your hands and legs. Don't tighten up.

If you are going to ride in a small enclosure, you can get along without assistance, but it is nice to have someone to help you teach the horse to go forward in response to leg signals. Perhaps all that will be needed is a squeeze of your legs and a cluck of your tongue. If the horse does not understand, ask a friend to lead the horse for you. Practice starting and stopping, traveling short distances in between, and standing quietly for a minute or so after each halt. Use your legs before your friend starts the horse forward, and soon the horse will answer your legs alone. When that happens, you will no longer need assistance.

If you are going to start riding on a longe line, you will need the help of someone who is familiar with longeing techniques. An individual who has never handled a longe line and whip might frighten the horse, and certainly will not know what to do if trouble occurs. As an alternative, find a capable volunteer to ride the horse while *you* handle the longe line. When working a horse on a longe line, the person who is holding the line and whip can help the rider teach the horse to answer leg signals to go forward. The line should be attached to a halter placed over or under the bridle or hackamore.

Handling the Reins

In this early stage of training, the reins must be held in two hands, regardless of the future work that is planned for the horse. If you want to teach your horse to neck-rein, wait until he has learned to carry a rider in good balance.

The reins should be slightly limp at all times except when they are used to signal the horse to turn or reduce pace. They should not be dangling loosely, but neither should they be stretched in contact with the bit or bosal. If they are too loose, the horse is free to jump out of control. If they are held in close contact, they will worry the young horse and inhibit his movement. The only kind of contact you should maintain might be described as "light contact by the weight of the reins."

Riders who are interested in jumping and dressage sometimes have the mistaken notion that they should start riding colts on elastic and positive "soft contact" with a snaffle bit to "give them support." However, young horses must learn to go forward with confidence and stability before they can be taught to accept this kind of contact correctly. If they are asked to "accept the bit" too soon, before they can be *ridden forward* onto contact, they are very likely to develop habits of faulty carriage, because any "support" their riders attempt to give them can be offered only by pulling back on the reins.

Never, at any stage of training, should a horse be ridden on constant and positive contact with a curb bit or bosal.

While practicing walking and halting in the small enclosure, think of the way you use your hands. Apply the lessons you learned in ground driving. Do not pull the horse to a halt. *Signal* him to halt with resisting hands. You will know that you are pulling if there is *any change* in the position of the horse's head before he halts. When there is head displacement, then it means that the reins are not acting "through the horse" as they should. Remember, also, that if you are using a bit and the horse's mouth opens wide, it is because of pulling.

This point is very difficult to get across to riders who always have depended on pulling to stop their horses. They have used pulling so much that they do not believe it is dispensable. Typically, one rider told me: "I've read books but they are not realistic. They say you shouldn't pull. But they don't seem to allow for the fact that sometimes horses will not answer soft-handed signals, especially when they are excited. I know from experience that sometimes you have to get tough and *make* a horse stop. And the only way to do that is by pulling." The rider was correct in stating that sometimes you have to get tough to make a horse stop, but incorrect in saying that the only way to do it is by pulling. There is another way to get tough when it is necessary, and if you can understand it and learn to do it, then you will never need to pull. All expert horsemen know how to do it. They don't really have "magic" in their hands. They just know how to exercise authority without engaging in an argument of pulling.

Let's assume, at first, that you are riding with a snaffle bit. What is the signal for the halt? In line-driving, when you were walking behind the horse, you simply slowed your pace and let the horse encounter resistance from your hands. Now, when you are in the saddle, you cannot slow *your* pace, but you can simulate the situation. Take the slack out of the reins, feel the horse's mouth, and then apply tension. If the signal causes the horse to hesitate, reward him by relaxing the tension for a moment, then repeat the signal. He probably will halt on the second signal. When he does, relax the reins instantly.

But what do you do if the horse does *not* yield to the tension on the reins? What if he ignores your signal and starts pulling against you? The answer to this is that you do not give him your two hands to pull against. Maintain firm contact with one hand, and tug backward with the other hand, in one swift and smooth "take-and-release" motion. You must do this with sufficient authority to "bring the horse back off your hands." It is important to tug only with one rein, and to keep contact with the other rein. *The other rein keeps the head from turning in response to the tug.*

This action of one rein to break up resistance can be very subtle, and it usually is subtle when a horse is only walking, or it can be severe, as it should be on a runaway horse. In more advanced schooling, when a horse is well trained on soft contact on a snaffle, the one-handed action is refined to a gesture of merely opening and closing the fingers of the hand, so that the horse is reminded that he has nothing to set his mouth against. At the other extreme, sometimes the only way to stop a headstrong horse is by planting one hand firmly on the crest of the horse's neck and using the other hand powerfully to "set the horse down." Jockeys often do this. They know that pulling with both hands won't stop their horses, because their horses are taught to "take hold of the bit and go."

As soon as the horse is "brought back to hand" with one rein, repeat the original signal. If you have done your part well, you will find that the horse will be prepared to halt at the first suggestion of tension on both reins. He will be mentally prepared, because you have told him to "pay attention" to your hands, and he will be physically prepared, because you will have caused him to shift his balance rearward.

Incidentally, the one-rein action will not work "through the horse" to shift his balance rearward if it is applied when the horse's head is out of normal position. Therefore, if you find that you have waited too long to use it, and the nose is raised high or is tucked into the chest, the best thing to do is relax both reins for a moment (stop pulling) and let the horse go forward on a light rein until his head position is restored. Then try again. In an emergency, when a horse has his head too low and his nose tucked inward, you can use a short *lifting* action on one rein to get the head up and the nose out before applying the rein rearward.

Using a one-rein action to break up resistance is not as easy as it may sound, because it requires a certain ability to feel what is happening to a horse's balance. Riders who try but cannot grasp the technique need not despair. They can hope that with more experience the time will come when they will be ready to graduate from "pulling hands." However, such riders should use only the snaffle bit in starting young horses under saddle, and they should proceed slowly in schooling in order to avoid wrestling matches with their horses' mouths.

Anyone who uses a bosal in starting a young horse *must* understand and learn quickly to use the one-rein action, because this is the only checking action that should be used from the saddle, at least in early riding. When line-driving a colt from the ground with a bosal, it acts only across the nose, like a rigid halter. However, when riding with a bosal, action on the reins lifts the heel knot and brings curb pressure against the lower jaw. Tension and resistance therefore cause the bosal to grip the horse's nose, and *the bosal was not invented for the purpose of locking and holding a horse's nose in a vise.* In fact, to ensure that there is never any prolonged gripping of the nose, the one-rein action should be less a "tug" than a little "bump." This is why a large, stiff bosal is used at first on colts—it is made for "bumping." After the young horse has learned to answer it lightly, it is exchanged for a smaller, more flexible bosal. A horse that is well trained on a bosal comes to respond to a whisper of the reins. A horse that is badly trained on a bosal, by a rider who pulls and who asks too much too soon, develops sores and bumps on the nose and under the jaw, and understandably becomes difficult to control.

In the hands of a trainer who knows how to use it, the bosal is an excellent piece of equipment. Some people think it is pointless to start a horse on a bosal, when a bit will be used later anyway, to school the horse in collection. However, the great advantage of the bosal is that it cannot even accidentally harm the horse's *mouth* or cause mouth problems to develop while the young horse is learning his simple basic lessons of carrying a rider. And any horse that learns to respond to "a whisper of the reins" with a bosal will quickly learn to respond with equal readiness to the bit.

Thus far, the discussion has centered on using the reins to halt the horse. How are they used for turning? Just as you used them in line-driving, except that at first you must not expect the horse to be as responsive to signals from the saddle as he was to signals from the ground. Give him all the help he needs. Make the turns wide and gradual, and "lead" him through them, if necessary, by extending your active hand out to one side. Take care not to unconsciously restrain him with the other hand.

As in line-driving, once you have applied tension on one rein as a signal to turn, wait for the horse to do the turning. Don't be impatient and pull his head to one side. Let him discover that by turning he finds relief from the tension, and he soon will be turning in response to a mere suggestion of tension. Use your legs, as needed, to keep him moving through the turns.

Once your horse seems agreeable to going forward at a walk, turning, halting, and standing quietly, take him outside the small enclosure and ride him at a walk in a large arena. If he is somewhat nervous, you will find it extremely helpful to ride alongside or behind a friend on a quiet, well-mannered older horse. The young horse will be reassured by the attitude of the older horse. Conversely, it is better to ride alone than with a friend on an excitable horse. In their natural state, horses survive through herd instinct. When one throws his head up and snorts fearfully, all become frightened. If he bolts away, the others stampede after him. Your young horse is still very close to nature. It will be a while, yet, before you can be sure that he is conditioned to trust you over and above instinct.

CHAPTER X

Establishing Basic Controls

Even when a young horse has been carefully conditioned to accept his introduction to the experience of being ridden, there is no certainty that everything will go smoothly. During his first few workouts under saddle, there always is a possibility that he might unexpectedly become frightened and start to "act up." If this happens before you have had time to acquaint the horse with your hand and leg controls, you may not be able to prevent a sudden act of violence, but you must make every effort to see to it that he wins nothing by the act.

Remember that if your colt does become frightened the odds are in your favor that he will not panic. He may jump or shy, but you probably will be able to steady him, because he has learned to trust you. As soon as he is under control, resume work as though nothing has happened. He will be reassured by your attitude and yield to your authority—if you seem to be sure of yourself.

What if you are not entirely confident when difficulties arise? If nothing else, try not to betray your insecurity to the horse. Regardless of your instincts, observe these rules:

1. Do not tighten the grip of your hands and legs. This will only increase the horse's fear, and it will make your muscles rigid. Concentrate on keeping yourself physically relaxed and supple, so that you can respond athletically to the horse's movements, and do what is necessary to regain control.

2. Do not pat and soothe the horse during or immediately after misbehavior, even when the misbehavior, such as shying or rearing, results from anxiety. All too often, a novice rider takes "time

out" to do this in an attempt to calm and reassure his horse, when it would be much more reassuring for him to ignore the misbehavior and gently but firmly put the horse back to work. Patting and soothing, *accompanied by an interruption of work*, can be interpreted by the horse as evidence of uncertainty and timidity on the part of the rider, and this can increase the horse's anxiety. It also can be interpreted by the horse as a pleasant consequence of his misbehavior, and can lead to his use of shying or rearing as a device to evade work. If you are a confident rider and can pat and soothe an anxious horse *while smoothly regaining and maintaining control*, you may do so. Generally, however, it is best to save the patting and soothing for gestures of approval, or for reassuring a horse that is nervous but is *not* misbehaving.

3. Do not dismount unless in imminent danger. Dismounting is the maximum reward that can be given to a horse. If you feel that you must dismount (as when a horse begins to misbehave where the footing is slippery), then do so, but remount as quickly as possible, and then stay on the horse until you can dismount as a reward for *good* behavior.

Sometimes even the best of riders dismounts accidentally. Falling off is rougher on you than dismounting on purpose, but it adds up to the same thing to the horse—maximum reward. Unless you are injured, or must take a moment to arrange for precautions against a recurrence of the accident, you should try to get back in the saddle before the horse realizes what has happened.

If you are afraid to remount the horse after a fall, use good judgment. Being afraid is no disgrace unless you are immature enough to think it so. A little fear can be a healthy thing. It makes the senses keen, and quickens responses. Too much fear can be paralyzing. If you are very much afraid, then it may be a mistake for you to try to give your horse his critical first few rides. You are accustomed to handling and controlling the horse from the ground, so why not longe the horse with someone else on his back? Or saddle an older, well-trained horse and "pony" your colt with a rider? The practice of "ponying" young horses, or leading them from horseback during their introduction to riding, is routine among many professional trainers, particularly those who specialize in high-strung stock.

Using a Riding Crop

At this early stage in riding, there should be no thought of punishing the young horse for erratic behavior. Plainly, it would make no sense to punish him for doing something "wrong," when he doesn't even know what is "right." Inflicting pain can only compound his fears and stir resentment.

You should, however, carry a riding crop, not as an instrument for punishment of misbehavior, but as an aid in conditioning the horse to go forward in response to a light squeeze of your legs. As you will recall from the previous chapter, once your horse is conditioned to go forward, you will be able to prevent or thwart most problems of misbehavior.

The riding crop should be a crop, and not a limber whip or quirt. Again it is appropriate to mention a point made earlier: The crop is relatively inflexible, and can be used with more wrist action than shoulder action; therefore, it is never necessary to swing it wide to tap the horse. In effect, it extends the reach of the rider's arm, and can be used with subtlety and precision. Cultivate a habit of holding and using the crop "invisibly." Carry it in your right hand, with the butt of the handle pointed approximately toward the horse's left ear, and the crop itself resting across your right thigh. When using the crop, keep your hand low and close to the horse. Riders who wave their crops carelessly in the air, and swing them widely in use, invariably teach their horses to react anxiously to the sight of the crop. This is extremely undesirable.

The crop is used whenever necessary to reinforce signals from the rider's legs. At times, while a horse is learning his new job of carrying a rider, he will fail to respond promptly to leg signals to go forward. Whenever this happens with your horse, do not increase the pressure of your legs, and do not kick. Tap the horse with the crop to stimulate him to react correctly. Otherwise he might, like so many children's ponies, become sluggishly tolerant of squeezing legs and pummeling heels.

Teaching horses to answer light signals from the legs is a matter of pride to fine horsemen. It is easier said than done, in the cases of riders who cannot or will not think about it enough to condition themselves always to use their legs lightly when riding. Admittedly, it is very difficult for someone to "think about it enough" if he is quite young, or if he is a beginning rider preoccupied with his own safety, or if he is a rider with a longtime habit of using his legs heavily.

The first time you use your crop on your horse, you may have to reach far back and tap him on the rump (not in the ticklish flank) to help him understand that it is a signal to go forward. He should get the idea quickly because it will be natural for him to want to escape the little attack from behind. He is unlikely to be frightened by the crop, because he is accustomed to your use of the longe whip to send him forward. Still, keep yourself well in the saddle. If the horse is startled and kicks up or jumps a little, tap him again, more insistently, to repeat your order to go forward. Never reward a kick or jump by ceasing the use of the crop. This would make it appear to the horse that he had responded correctly, and would encourage him to react in the same way the next time he felt the crop. (Perhaps now you can understand why so many timid riders have horses that "get mad" when they use the crop. And perhaps you can figure out how circus trainers teach their horses to do the "rhumba.")

Once the horse understands that the crop tells him to go forward, start using it inconspicuously on his side, behind your leg, instead of reaching back to the rump. And always use it only as a correction of failure to respond promptly to a signal from the legs.

Here is further advice on this important subject: Never pull back on the reins while using the crop. Novice riders often pull on one or both reins, quite unconsciously, when they reach back with their crops to try to drive their horses forward. When you are going to bring the crop into action, "bridge" the reins into one hand to free the hand that is holding the crop. If you do not know how to do this smoothly and swiftly, then practice and learn how to do it. Your horse *must* be allowed to go forward freely when he feels the crop, else he will be confused and justly annoyed by the contradictory signals.

Why not use spurs instead of a crop? Because, no matter how

blunt the spurs may be, their pricking is almost certain to cause a young horse to react by switching his tail, either before or when he starts forward. The tail-switching is a reflexive action that can quickly become a nervous habit, and nervous habits are extremely difficult to overcome. If spurs are used at all on a horse, they should be used only after the horse is fully trained, and then only for show purposes, when the rider wants to have an almost invisible means of correction of any failure to answer the legs. Skillful use of spurs on a mature horse after he is well trained to go forward is not as likely to cause him to be a tail-switcher, because he is not under the pressure of uncertainty and anxiety that is experienced by the green colt. However, when spurs are used crudely and as weapons of punishment, they can cause any horse to become a tail-switcher or even a tail-wringer. A tail-wringing horse is one that spasmodically whips its tail in a circular motion when under stress. It is not uncommon for the act to be accompanied by involuntary urination. The habit is unsightly and incurable, and of course indicates that a horse has been badly misused. It renders a horse all but valueless.

If you do not use spurs, chances are minimal that you will have any problems with tail-switching. However, if tail-switching *does* make an appearance, and seems to be developing into a habit, it means that you are doing *something* that the horse finds irritating. Note what specific act on your part incites the switching. Are you pestering and crowding the horse with your legs and heels, instead of using the crop correctly? Or are you annoying the horse with the crop, by using it in a way he cannot understand? Find out what you are doing wrong, and change your approach.

Dealing with Balkiness

There is another problem that might appear in early schooling. At its inception, it may seem relatively insignificant, because it is nonviolent, but it deserves your most serious attention. If your horse ever offers the slightest suggestion of balkiness, do something about it, and quickly. Do not ignore it, because it can become a vice in an incredibly short time. If you appreciate the importance of teaching a horse to go forward readily, it should be easy for you to understand why this is one problem that cannot be tolerated.

No matter how subtle a first hint of balkiness may be, it will be felt by the rider. It is an unmistakably deliberate refusal to comply with an order to go forward, when there is no apparent reason for hesitation. (Even well-trained horses may hang back for an instant when frightened, but that does not mean they are balky.) When beginning riders experience balkiness in their horses, their reaction is frustration. Invariably, they start pumping up and down in their saddles, as though they think their movement will inspire co-operation in their horses. Invariably, the pumping has no effect. Their horses obey them only when they decide they want to move. If and when you feel a suggestion of balkiness in your young horse, don't waste time pumping. React instantly by using your heels or your crop or any means at your disposal to *jolt* him forward, and give him free rein to go forward. It doesn't matter if this excites him. In fact, if it does, you can be sure you have made an impression on him. By vigorously attacking balkiness before it can take root as a habit, you can eliminate the problem altogether.

As you may know, a horse that already has a habit of balkiness cannot be handled in this way. Any efforts to jolt him forward are unlikely to succeed, because he will have learned to tolerate roughness. A truly balky horse sinks into a stupor whenever forceful tactics are employed. An expert horseman may be able to ride him, by tactfully working around the tendency to "sulk," but he will not be able to rid the horse of the idea of rebelling by balking. How does he work around the vice? By resisting the temptation to apply pressure the instant he feels the horse "hang up," and by urging the horse forward only when he senses that the horse is thinking of moving. Sometimes he makes a little game of outfiguring the horse. When he feels the horse is about to balk, he pulls back on the reins and stops him with a loud, "Whoa." By taking the initiative he bewilders the horse, and he may even add to the confusion by refusing to accept an offer to go forward. He allows the horse to go forward only when he is sure that the horse is not only willing but eager to do so, to escape the baffling situation. After a few such games, an expert can gain control of a balky horse.

All this emphasis on the correct handling of early difficulties is necessary because, as pointed out at the beginning of this book, training is a two-sided task. It involves more than simply teaching a horse *good* habits. The greater challenge in early schooling is in seeing to it that the horse does not learn *bad* habits.

Assuming now that your horse has learned to allow you to mount him and ride him at a walk in an arena, the next step is to teach him to carry you quietly and steadily at a trot. Even if you are a smooth and easy rider, your movement on his back at this gait is going to feel strange to the horse at first. If you tend to bounce, it will feel downright weird. This new sensation, together with the increase of speed, will tend to excite the horse. Your job is to try to minimize the excitement.

One thing you can do to minimize the excitement is return to the small enclosure or to the longe line for the introduction of trotting. The evidence of close control gives the young horse a sense of security. If you want to work in a large arena, enlist the aid of a friend on a quiet horse. The friend can ride alongside you to give your horse confidence, or can "pony" your horse for you.

Although ponying usually is unnecessary with a young horse that has been taught controls through line-driving, it can be a help with high-tempered colts. The person who rides the ponying horse should be an experienced horseman, capable of controlling his own horse *and* the young horse in moments of difficulty. His horse should be calm-natured and reliable, unlikely to be bothered by the buffeting antics of a colt. The pony rider will need a stock saddle, so that he can "snub" the young horse by a dally of the halter rope around his saddle horn if necessary. If he has never ponied a horse before, he should be cautioned about handling the lead rope and about using it for snubbing. He must not allow the rope to become caught to his saddle or himself. A halter rope caught fast can create an extremely dangerous situation. In an emergency, the pony rider should drop the halter rope rather than allow it to become caught. (A young horse should never be ponied with a halter alone. The rider must have his own means of control.)

When a young horse is to be ponied, he should first be led from horseback while unmounted. It will be easier then for the pony rider to assure himself of control, because neither he nor the colt will be worried about a rider on the colt's back. After control has been established the colt can be mounted.

Ponying will only be a nuisance if your colt does not need it, so don't adopt the practice solely because you have seen others do it.

Introducing the Trot

The best thing you can do to minimize excitement about trotting for the first time is to let it seem to "just happen." Instead of urging your horse to lurch from a walk into a trot, ask him to walk faster and faster, until he slips into a trot of his own volition. He may trot only a few steps, then drop back to a walk. If so, this a good sign. It indicates that he is not upset. Don't press him back into a trot immediately. Remember that cessation of demand is a reward. After a while, ask for a trot again, in the same way. If he remains calm, use your legs a little to keep him trotting for a short distance, then permit him (or encourage him) to walk again. That is all the trotting he needs on his first day.

In the second trotting lesson, concentrate on asking him to maintain the trot for longer distances. If you are working on a longe line, and the horse is trotting calmly, the circle should be as large as possible. Small circles would be difficult for him with a rider, because they require better balance and more effort. However, if your horse becomes excited and you want to slow his pace, you can induce him to do so by making small circles. Sometimes it is better to slow an excited horse in this manner than to engage in too much busy-work with the reins.

If it so happens that while trotting the horse "humps up" or "crow-hops" a little, because of the odd feeling on his back, make as little of it as possible. Don't pull back on the reins and stop him—that would give him a chance to gather himself for serious bucking. Just leave the reins light and nudge him onward.

(You may have heard that a rider should pull a horse's head up if he starts to buck hard. This is true, but there is more to it than simply yanking upward on the reins. A skilled rider uses a sharp lifting action on one rein not only to get the horse's head up, but also to get his *nose poked out*. Then he rocks back on the rein to *force the horse's back to hollow*. Instantly, he drives the horse forward. In this very awkward posture, the horse cannot buck. His head is up, his spine is hollowed, and the hind legs are "trailing." The "humping up" that a horse does when he thinks of bucking occurs because he is getting his hind legs under himself for lift-off. Horses are, as we've said, rear-engined animals.)

Chances are, if you have brought your horse along carefully, he will not try to buck hard. After two or three days of trotting, take him off the longe line or out of the small enclosure and include trotting in his daily workout in the large arena.

Your first objective when schooling at the trot will be to teach the horse to maintain a steady rate of speed. Find a rate that seems to be natural and easy for the horse. If you try to make the horse trot too slowly, in order to make yourself comfortable, you will find that you will have to check him constantly, and this nagging annoyance will cause him to start fighting the bit or bosal. It could make him into a head-tosser. A green colt cannot be expected to jog slowly. If he is calm, as he should be, then he will be naturally "slumped forward," carrying the bulk of his weight on the forehand. This causes him to spill forward, as though moving on a downhill grade, and he has to trot at least fast enough to keep up with his balance. In order to hold a very slow trot, he would have to shift and hold his balance rearward. Of course, he *can* shift his balance rearward, but in nature he does it only temporarily, when he wants to carry himself lightly to be ready for action, and usually he does it only when he is excited. He hasn't learned yet that he should shift his balance rearward and carry himself lightly under a rider at all times, even when he is calm. That will come later.

You will not have to worry about your horse trotting too slowly, but you will have to prevent him from going *too* fast. He may have a tendency to trot faster and faster until he breaks into a canter. So the question is: How fast is too fast? This is easy enough to determine. When a young horse is spilling forward at the trot and nears the "breaking point" of his gait, he becomes noticeably anxious. His breathing quickens and his stride becomes hasty and uneven. Regulate your horse's speed so that he stays under this anxiety level.

Schooling Figures

In order to avoid using the reins excessively, use turning movements more than checking with your hands to regulate speed. As you ride around the arena, following the track along the rail, you will note that your horse always spills forward and picks up speed on the "long sides" of the arena. Instead of checking with your hands, ride through "schooling figures" such as circles, half-circles, and figure eights. Make the figures large enough to be easy on the horse, but small enough to slow his pace. (Circles should not be smaller than twenty feet in diameter at this stage.) After the trot has been slowed, return to the track. Over a period of several days, the horse will learn to "lock in" to a steady rate of speed around the arena.

The schooling figures should be ridden accurately. Let's say you are riding down the track on one side of the arena, and decide to make a circle. Note the point at which you leave the track to start the circle, and make the circle perfectly round, returning to the track at the point of departure. Be conscientious about it. It isn't fair to the horse to ride irregular figures—how can he be expected to stabilize his balance and speed if you guide him on wavering lines?

A half-circle, sometimes called a half-turn, is a simple figure. In effect, all you do is turn the horse around to go in the opposite direction. To ride it smoothly and correctly, leave the track as though starting a full circle. When you are halfway around the circle, headed in the opposite direction, ride a diagonal line back to the track and continue on the track.

For variety, ride half-circles in reverse, or "backward." Veer off the track on a diagonal line to a point about twenty or thirty feet out from the track, then make a half-circle back to the track. Remember that both the half-circle and the half-circle-in-reverse are ways of turning around to go in the opposite direction.

In all your workouts, see to it that your horse gets an equal amount of practice in turning to the right and to the left. If you unconsciously favor one direction in turning, then he will begin to favor it. Of course, you can break the rule about equal practice if the horse seems to resist turning in one direction. Give him *more* practice on the difficult side.

The figure eight should not be ridden as a "lazy eight" but as two perfect circles. Always start a figure eight from the center of the eight, where the two circles join, and it will be easier for you to ride it accurately. For this figure, you will have to leave the track entirely. You may want to turn into the center of the arena to do it.

These figures will be good for your horse in several ways. They will help him to learn to turn, they will help to steady his trot, and they will lend variety to his schooling. A young horse can become bored quickly by doing nothing but walking and trotting around the track of an arena, and boredom can lead to irritability, and that can lead to trouble. So use the schooling figures freely and with imagination. Try making large circles and spiraling inward gradually to smaller circles, then unwinding gradually. In your figure eights, ride the circles two or three times before changing directions. When making half-circles, and half-circles-in-reverse, try doing two or three at a time, one immediately following the other.

What kind of schooling schedule should you plan for your horse? Generally, you might think in terms of spending an hour a day on him in the arena, but not *working* the entire hour. Intersperse his work with frequent and generous rest periods. The rest periods can consist of walking quietly on a loose rein, if the horse is overheated, or of standing idly. At first, the actual working time should be rather short. Start with a total of about twenty minutes per session, and add five minutes a day until you build up to forty minutes. When a young horse is not accustomed to schooling, intensive lessons can tire him mentally as well as physically, and can extinguish his desire to go forward.

In basic training, schooling in the confinement of an arena is not nearly as good for the young horse as riding him across country and putting "mileage" on him. There is nothing like travel to habituate a green colt to going forward without any fuss. The only reason you are working in an arena now is to establish basic controls, so that you can safely start trail-riding.

The rest periods that you give your horse while schooling in the arena can, in themselves, serve a training purpose. It will be extremely beneficial to him to have practice in "doing nothing" for five or ten minutes at a time while a rider is on his back. It will teach him to relax when he is not working. Horses that are never given a moment's peace by their riders come to associate being mounted with being active. They are particularly bad about fidgeting and pawing the ground when they are supposed to be standing still. So do a lot of "sitting around" on your horse. This is not unlike the training that you gave him in standing tied. You let him become accustomed to it through practice.

Incidentally, if your horse starts developing a tendency to move around restlessly while being mounted, it probably will be because *you* have a tendency to ask or permit him to go forward the moment you are in the saddle. He associates being mounted with going to work. You can eliminate that association by making it a habit of your own to require the horse to stand in place for two or three minutes or more *after* he is mounted. No matter how long it takes, if he is restless to go forward, outwait the restlessness.

Of course, clumsy riders have several other ways of making their horses restless about mounting, but it is assumed here that when you are mounting you do not commit clumsy errors. You do not accidentally pull on the reins, jab your toe into the horse, wrestle with the saddle, or take your seat heavily.

Posting at the Trot

Returning now to the subject of riding at the trot, something should be said about making it easy on yourself and the horse. Your horse's trot will be rough, because it will be fairly fast, and the horse will be heavy on the forehand. Whether you ride Western or "English," you will be more comfortable if you post the trot at this stage.

In former times, Western trainers avoided schooling at the trot until after their horses learned to carry themselves in good balance at the canter. They then taught their colts a slow jog. They never "moved out" at the trot. As a consequence, the little jog usually was peggy and stiff. Now, however, most of the better Western trainers introduce trotting early, and they post at the trot while it is rough. They feel that schooling at the "long trot" helps a horse learn to "use himself" efficiently. Later, when the slow jog is introduced, it is more likely to be supple and silky.

When posting at the trot, the rider rises and returns to the saddle in rhythm with the movement of the horse. He rises on alternating strides. As you probably know, when a horse is trotting, his legs move in diagonal pairs, and for this reason the trot is said to be a two-beat movement. The left foreleg and the right hind leg move forward as one diagonal pair, and the right foreleg and left hind leg as the other.

In this country, many horsemen believe that it is desirable for a rider to make it a practice always to "post the outside diagonal" when his horse is turning. This means that the rider should be rising when the outside foreleg is reaching forward. In other words, when a horse is turning to the *left*, the rider should be rising when the *right* foreleg is reaching forward. Thus, he will be out of the saddle when the outside foreleg and the inside hind leg are off the ground. He will be in the saddle when the outside foreleg and inside hind leg are *on* the ground. The point that is often put forth is that it is easier for the rider to influence the horse when he is down in the saddle, and he can be most influential when the inside hind leg is on the ground. Also, the rider's weight will be off the already burdened inside front leg and there will be better balance.

In reality, whether you post the inside diagonal or the outside diagonal through turns is relatively unimportant in basic training. *It is important only that you see to it that the horse has an equal amount of work on both diagonals.* If you do not think about diagonals at all, you will always post the same diagonal, and your horse may develop an uneven way of going. He will become one-sided about posting and will travel clumsily when he has a rider who takes up the "wrong" diagonal.

The easiest way to remember to divide the work on the diagonals in an arena is to adopt the habit of posting on one diagonal when going one way around the track, and the other diagonal when going the other way. If you plan to ride in hunter or saddle horse classes in horse shows, you might as well accustom yourself to posting the outside diagonal on the rail and through turns, for that is expected in horse shows in the United States. When you travel on long straight stretches across country, you will have to make it a point to think of changing diagonals at regular intervals. Changing diagonals at the trot and changing leads at the canter refresh a horse in distance riding, because the practice relieves some muscles while it brings others into action.

As your horse's trot becomes steady through daily schooling, you will find that his walk begins to improve. Most young horses walk clumsily and stumble frequently during their early riding. The calmer they are, the more they stumble. This, too, is a result of heaviness on the forehand. Your young horse at first will have no sense of purpose in walking forward under a rider, and, on the flat surface of the arena, no apparent need to carry himself athletically. The work at the trot will help keep him awake. However, riding on uneven terrain across country will be even more helpful. This is another reason why you will not want to dwell too long on schooling in the arena.

Unless you are insensitive to the quality of a horse's gaits, a clumsy walk will be somewhat frustrating, but it is no real cause for worry at present. The fact that the horse is calm is a good sign. The thing to worry about, if it makes an appearance, is restless prancing at the walk. This will be a sign of nervousness, and you should waste no time in discovering and eliminating the cause. It cannot be repeated too often that nervous habits are the most difficult to cure.

Causes of Prancing

Most commonly, restless prancing occurs in young horses for these reasons: 1. The reins are kept too short or are held too tightly, preventing a relaxed carriage of the head and neck. 2. The rider makes rapid-fire requests for changes of pace, as though he can't make up his mind what he wants to do. 3. The rider, when in the company of a friend on horseback, lets the young horse get the idea that he is supposed to keep up with the other horse. When the rider tries to hold him back, the young horse starts prancing.

The rule about the reins is to keep them long and light, so that the horse can keep his neck long and straight, as he naturally does when he is calm. If your horse is sensitive about the bit or bosal, you may have the reins too short without realizing it. They may not feel "tight" to you, because the horse is not pressing against your hands, but the horse may be holding his head back in an unnatural position to *avoid* pressing against your hands. If you suspect that you are inhibiting the head carriage, feed out the reins and allow the horse to lengthen and lower his neck. This may be all that is required to eliminate nervous prancing.

Perhaps you are wondering just how high or how low the horse's head should be. This will depend to some extent on the horse's conformation, but you do not have to be an expert to make the determination. If you see to it that he moves calmly on a light rein, with his neck long and relaxed, he will show you how high his head should be. There is a possibility, of course, that he will become so relaxed and calm that he will drop his head too low. If his head nods downward until his poll is below the level of his withers, it means that he is falling asleep on the job. Don't try to correct this by pulling his head up. Awaken him with your legs.

Rapid-fire requests for changes of pace are unnerving to a young horse. They keep him guessing about what's coming next, and this leads to fitful prancing. In your very diligence as a trainer, or from boredom at working in an arena, you may have a tendency to change signals too often. Restrain yourself. Let the horse settle into his work.

While schooling in an arena, you probably will not ride alongside other horses to any great extent. When you do, make it a point *not* to allow your horse to change pace of his own accord to keep abreast of other horses. Your horse must learn to increase or decrease pace only when you signal him to do so. To instill obedience in this matter, give your horse little practice sessions. Ask friends to ride alongside you for a while at a walk, then let them go on ahead at a trot while you continue to walk. Also, practice leaving them behind while you move ahead. Later, when you are riding across country with friends, don't let yourself get caught up in group psychology. If someone suddenly kicks his horse into a canter, and other riders follow suit, let them go on ahead for a bit before putting your horse into a canter. If your horse prances and frets, don't canter at all. Turn around and go the other way, if that is what it takes to settle him and convince him that he takes his cues only from you. After he is calm, you can overtake your friends at a trot. This kind of training is invaluable. If a horse is not allowed to become herd-bound, and thus does not *expect* to keep up with other horses, then he will not prance when he is left behind.

Introducing the Canter

When will your horse be ready to start schooling at the canter? As soon as he has learned to walk without excitement, and to maintain a trot without spilling forward *accidentally* into a canter. If he is calm-natured, he may be ready for the canter after only a few days of walking and trotting. If he is high-strung, he may need more time. Give him all the time he needs, but don't delay unnecessarily. Remember that you want to graduate him to trail-riding as soon as possible.

To introduce the canter, use your own judgment about safety precautions. If you feel that there is a chance that your horse will overreact with excitement, you can return to the small enclosure, providing it allows you to ride a circle at least fifty feet in diameter, or you can return to the longe line. Don't try to ride the horse at a canter on too small a circle. It would be difficult for him to maintain pace.

You can introduce the canter in the large arena if you are satisfied that the schooling at the walk and trot has given you a reasonable degree of control. In the large arena, it will be easier for him to slip into the canter and hold it.

To minimize any excitement in starting the canter for the first time, wait until the end of a regular schooling session to ask for it, so that your horse will not have a surplus of fresh energy. As you did when you started the trot, let the canter seem to "just happen." Ease the horse into a faster and faster trot until he rolls into a canter. If you do it this way, he will be a little surprised but probably not frightened, and he will canter only a few strides and then drop back to a trot. Let him trot for a while, making certain that he is calm before you ask for the canter again. The second time he canters, he may hold it a little longer, with gentle encouragement. Whether he does or not, show him that you are pleased with him by ceasing work for the day.

It is *possible* that your horse will show his surprise when he first canters by bucking a little. If so, remember to leave the reins light and nudge him onward.

It is also possible, although unlikely, that your horse will become frightened, and, instead of dropping back to a trot after a few strides, may start picking up speed. If this happens, and he fails to respond to a checking signal, don't try to wrestle him to a stop. That would only add to his fear. Concentrate more on guiding him than on trying to stop him. If you are in the arena, guide him into a large circle at one end of the arena and let him keep going on the circle. His excitement will give way to weariness, and you can regain control without a battle. He will not feel that he has won anything, for he will not even know that you were temporarily helpless. However, do not cease work immediately after such an incident. Walk him a while to cool and calm him, then try the canter again. There is almost no chance that he will become headstrong the second time.

If you elect to introduce the canter in a small enclosure or on the longe line, spend only a limited amount of time on it there. Constantly cantering on a circle under a rider is hard work for a young horse, and can be overdone all too easily. Incorporate cantering into your daily schooling program in the arena as soon as you feel you can do it safely.

Your objective in schooling at the canter will be to stabilize the canter on a light rein. The horse still will be heavy on the forehand, and his canter will seem rough and fast. Because of his balance, he will not be able to slow his pace much without breaking into a trot, so don't look for a rocking-chair canter. To keep him from going *too* fast and spilling into a gallop, ride large circles as necessary.

As yet, you should not be concerned about teaching the horse to understand specific signals for teaching leads at the canter, but you must see to it that he receives an equal amount of exercise on both leads. If you do not give him equal work on both leads, he will quickly develop a favored side. You can put him into either lead simply and naturally by easing him into the canter while he is trotting through a turn at one of the ends of the arena. When you are turning to the left, he will take the left lead, and vice versa. You will find that he misses a lead only when he is stiff and anxious. Therefore, when he does miss a lead, don't increase his anxiety by acting displeased. Check him smoothly back to a trot, get him settled, and try again.

If you have ridden in horse shows, you may think it rather primitive to put a horse into a canter by the method described above. You may be in the habit of checking a horse (bringing him back to hand) for a light canter depart. However, you cannot expect a young horse to lift himself lightly into a canter before he even knows how to canter lightly. Give him a chance to learn something about balance before you introduce sophistication into his schooling. Wait until after he has had his cross-country experience.

When the young horse has learned to canter without anxiety, he will be ready for cross-country riding.

Arena Behavior

In your work in the arena, try to avoid developing habits of your own that will teach undesired habits to your horse. If you find that the horse always seems to pick up speed at one place along the rail, it may be because you habitually ask for the canter in that place. If the horse always wants to cut across the ends of the arena, it may be because you carelessly allow him to do so most of the time. If he always wants to pull in to the center of the arena, it may be because you always ride to the center when you intend to let him rest. If he wants to stop when he encounters people along the rail, it may be because you often stop to talk to people. And if he always wants to stop at the gate, or wants to go out when the gate is open, it will be because you always ride directly out the gate when work is done.

To prevent any possibility of teaching your horse to be "gate-bound," make it a rule never to ride *directly* out the gate. If you want to ride out the gate, first ride past it, then turn around, and go out. However, it is better, when quitting work, to dismount somewhere inside the arena and then lead the horse out the gate. Unless there are other horses working in the arena, dismount somewhere along the rail, in a different place every time.

One thing that may trouble you in the course of your training of the horse will be unsteadiness in his rate of improvement. *Don't worry about progress from day to day; evaluate it from week to week.* Horses, like people, have good days and difficult days when they are learning new things. Enjoy the good days, and do the best you can on the others. (Unless you are inclined to be a perfectionist, the good days will far outnumber the rest.) Make allowances, also, for occasional and quite normal plateaus in the horse's learning progress.

Once in a great while there will be a lesson in which everything seems to go wrong from the start. It may be because the horse has decided to test your authority, but don't leap to that conclusion. Consider, first, the possibility that the horse may be unsettled or distressed for some reason. Are blustery winds distracting him? Is he coming down with a cold? Consider, also, the possibility that *you* may be unsettled or distressed for some reason. Are you angry about something, or feeling moody? If you feel certain that the horse has coolly decided to test your authority, then see the lesson through, but if there is a strong possibility that there are legitimate reasons for the problems, then give the horse the benefit of the doubt, and curtail the lesson. Give him a very light workout, and quit on a good note. Nothing will be lost by playing it safe for one day.

CHAPTER XI

Riding Cross-Country

If you want to avoid many unnecessary problems that other people have in training green young horses, now is the time to suspend the ritualistic work in the arena and start trail-riding. Your horse has been introduced to the signals to walk, trot, canter, turn, and halt. There is no better or more pleasant way to confirm those lessons than by taking him on excursions across country. Within only a few days, you will begin to see the results. Your horse will begin to accept riding as a matter of routine. However, the cross-country phase of his basic training should not be limited to a few days. The more "mileage" the horse is given under saddle, the better he will be prepared, when the time comes, to return to the arena and settle down to any specialty schooling that you may have in mind for him.

Some trainers cannot restrain themselves from trying to teach their young horses too much too soon, even when they know better and are not under any pressure to hurry. They want to leap ahead to "exciting" things, such as roll-backs and quick stops (if they are Western riders), or to jumping (if they work with hunters), or to collection (if they specialize in saddle horses). Here, I am not referring to novice trainers, but to *experienced* trainers, who find it boring to hack in the open. It would be better for their young horses if they could be turned over to competent but undemanding riders who would give them the simple ground-covering experience they need.

In helping novice trainers break in their own young horses, I have found that they rather enjoy the final basic training phase of "just plain riding." They don't think it boring, because even though they are not working on subtleties, they are still training. They undertake cross-country riding in the spirit of adventure, searching out streams and bridges to cross, hills and valleys to explore, and making it a point to acquaint their horses with the sights and sounds of motor traffic. Perhaps the best thing about it is that they realize a growing sense of partnership with their horses. *It is in cross-country work that young horses learn to go frankly forward, putting their faith in their riders.*

While writing this book, I received a letter from a sixteen-year-old girl in Illinois, who was having difficulty with a three-year-old filly she had raised. The filly had been started under saddle, but her training was at a standstill because she was developing a habit of rearing. She had reared and fallen with a professional trainer. The girl asked what to do about the problem.

The girl indicated that she had been given all the usual suggestions, but she did not know how to distinguish between the good and the bad. She had been told to punish the horse by striking it on the head whenever it attempted to rear; however, she said she did not want to be brutal, and quite rightly guessed that it would be risky to try to inflict such punishment. She had been told to use a martingale as a mechanical aid to prevent the horse from rearing, but she felt that she would rather solve the problem than disguise it. Finally, she had been told that she could prevent the horse from rearing by driving it forward. She realized that the last suggestion made sense, because a horse cannot rear while moving forward, but she said it was of no use in her case because her horse would not respond to her efforts to drive it forward at critical moments.

In my reply to the letter, I affirmed that the answer to the problem *did* lie in the maxim of driving the horse forward. If her horse did not allow himself to be driven forward, then she must *concentrate on teaching and conditioning the horse to go forward.* She must think of the rearing not as an isolated type of misbehavior but as a version of balkiness.

How could she concentrate on teaching the horse to go forward if it had already picked up the dangerous trick of rearing? The girl had said she did most of her riding alone in an arena, and so I suspected that the filly might be frustrated and soured by work in the enclosure. I recommended regular riding across country, in the company of friends on horseback. I added that the girl might consider using a martingale on the horse at first, as a defense against rearing, until the horse became conditioned to responding to the aids to go forward. (A martingale prevents a horse from throwing its head high, and thus inhibits rearing. A horse *can* rear while wearing a martingale, but it is somewhat difficult.)

Some months later, the girl wrote to tell me that she had followed the advice, and it worked. She had not used a martingale. Apparently, it was not needed. The filly seemed to enjoy "going places" cross-country, and had never reared again. She had learned to answer the rider's leg signals to go forward. Now she would work in an arena without difficulty, and was doing so well in her training that the girl planned to ride her in pleasure classes in shows the next summer.

If the rearing problem had been more fully confirmed as a vice, it might not have been so easily solved. It was fortunate that the young rider became thoughtfully concerned about it at an early stage.

Riding with Friends

The first few times you ride your young horse away from the stable, make every effort to see to it that the excursions are unexciting. Ride with a friend or friends on quiet horses, and *spend most or all of the time walking*. Avoid routes that would require the negotiation of steep inclines, or the crossing of highways, rattling bridges, deep water, or swampy ground. Remember that horses are instinctively fearful of uncertain footing.

Ask your friends to precede you over or past necessary obstacles. If a friend's horse balks at an obstacle ahead, turn your horse around and ride nonchalantly away. Don't let your horse become infected by the other's fear. If the other horses pass an obstacle, but your horse is afraid to follow, don't make an issue of it. Casually dismount and try to lead your horse to the others. If he still hangs back, ask your friends to continue on down the road—your horse will not want to be left behind. On your return, if by the same route, your horse will probably not hesitate at the obstacle. If he does, dismount again, and lead him. By doing this, you are not "babying" the horse. You are showing him there is nothing to fear. Later, when he is more experienced at traveling across country, you can be increasingly insistent on boldness.

At times, your horse may seem to be unreasonably afraid of minor obstacles. Don't be too quick to belittle his anxiety. Try to think of things *his* way. Is he reluctant to walk through an isolated little puddle of water? Well, why shouldn't he be? How does he know how deep the water is, or what lies beneath the surface? If he were running free, he would go around the puddle or leap over it. Don't expect him to forget his natural fears just because you are on his back. You are going to have to earn that kind of trust.

Trying to force a frightened young horse to walk through small puddles of water is an unnecessary exercise in frustration. It is all too easy for the horse to skirt the puddle by dancing sideways. Yet some riders seem to think it is a big thing—a test of wills. They say they aren't about to let their horses get the best of them "just because they don't want to get their feet wet." And so they engage in battle, and usually succeed only in teaching their horses to be forever shy of puddles. How much better it would be if they realized, as do trainers of jumpers, that it is unwise to try to force green horses over narrow obstacles that invite run-outs.

You probably will have no difficulty in crossing shallow, quiet streams if you closely follow another horse that is bold and unafraid. Be certain that you enter the water where the footing is good, and where there is no danger of stepping unexpectedly into a hole. You will not earn your horse's confidence if you ride him into trouble. If the water is clean, you can stop and offer to let the horse drink. However, if he starts pawing the water, *move him forward and keep going*. He may be thinking of lying down for a cool dip.

Although it is all right to allow your horse to drink water, make it a firm rule never to allow him to eat grass while you are on his back. Otherwise, he will develop the annoying habit of trying to pull the reins from your hands so he can put his head down and graze whenever you stop him in a likely spot. Children's ponies sometimes are so bad about this that they have to be fitted with overchecks to keep their heads up. If you want to allow your horse to graze, dismount first.

When riding alongside a road where there is motor traffic, take the precaution at first of positioning yourself so that there is another horse between yours and passing cars. If your horse shows no signs of fear, fall in behind the other horse. Keep your ears attuned to the approach of vehicles that make unusual sounds, such as lumbering trucks or motorcycles, for they might make even your friends' horses uneasy. If you are in doubt about any situation, move as far from the roadside as possible, but don't tighten the reins as though you expect trouble.

When you are ready to introduce trotting into your cross-country riding, take advantage of the terrain. At first, always start the trotting while moving on a slight but long uphill incline. If the horse has a tendency to trot too fast, you will not have to check him excessively. The uphill incline will settle him and keep his balance back. By the time he reaches level ground, he should be settled enough to maintain the same steady trot he learned in the arena. Don't trot him on downhill inclines for a while. In later riding, it will be good for him, for it will help him learn to shift his balance back in response to a check on the reins, but at present it would be asking too much of him.

Use the same tactic when introducing the canter, but remember that the uphill inclines should be slight. Cantering up steep grades is hard work for any horse. Consider how difficult it would be for you to run up a steep hill, particularly when carrying a burden.

Some trainers recommend riding through plowed fields or deep sand to slow the trot and canter of young horses. This is effective because it is tiring, but it can be overdone all too easily and can strain muscles and tendons.

As your horse becomes more and more sure of himself and of you, start breaking away from your dependence on staying alongside or behind other horses. When riding with friends, take the lead occasionally, or make little "side trips" on your own into the countryside and then rejoin them.

The next step will be to start taking cross-country rides by yourself. Even though you may be a sociable person who prefers to ride with friends, your horse needs the experience of going out alone. However, there is one more thing that it would be wise to do with your horse before you ride cross-country alone. You should introduce him to galloping, under carefully controlled conditions. There is a sound reason for doing this. Someday, when riding your young horse across country, he might be frightened into bolting. If he has been ridden at a gallop before, you will be able to regain control rather quickly, as soon as the initial panic subsides. If he has not been ridden at speed before, the very fact that he finds himself running will add to his fear.

Are you in any doubt about the difference between the canter and the gallop? When a horse is cantering, only three beats can be heard, because one diagonal pair of legs strikes the ground almost simultaneously. When a horse "stretches out" into a gallop, four beats are heard, because each of the four feet strikes the ground separately. A horse can gallop at various rates. When he is moving at a full gallop, he is moving at top speed, or, as some might say, "a dead run."

Introducing the Gallop

Galloping can be introduced within the confines of a large arena, but this is not necessary. It might even cause difficulties, because of the turns that must be negotiated. Usually, it is better to introduce galloping in open country, on carefully chosen terrain, where there is a long straight-of-way to travel. The ground should be firm but not hard, and free of holes and ditches. If you want everything in your favor, seek out a gentle upward incline. Level ground is all right, of course, but a downhill slope would pitch the horse forward and invite stumbling.

Although you should be accompanied by one or two friends on the day you plan your first gallop, the idea is *not* to gallop *with* them, but to take advantage of their presence in another way. First, take a long, quiet trail ride, to be sure that your horse is calm and settled. Then, *before you start homeward,* choose a place for your gallop. Ask your friends to stop and stay where they are, while you ride on ahead. Put your horse into a trot, then a canter. Then, gradually ease the horse into a controlled gallop (not a full gallop). The horse will not be frightened by it, if the transitions are smooth and unhurried. And you will have an ace up your sleeve—the horse will be aware that he is leaving the other horses behind, and that he is heading away from home; this will influence him to be agreeable when you check him. If for some reason the horse is *not* agreeable to slowing his pace when you first check him, don't fight him. Let him go on, even if he runs. It won't be long before he tires. When he offers to slow his pace, require him to gallop a few more strides, then check him, and he will respond. Walk back and rejoin your friends, or signal to them to come to you. There should be no more galloping in the first lesson.

After several days (not necessarily consecutive) of giving your horse brief experiences at galloping at a *controlled* rate, you can ease him into a full gallop once or twice, just to let him learn that it is no big thing. That will be all the practice he needs at running in the course of his basic training. Even if you plan later to train him in a specialty that requires speed, running him too much now would be a mistake. Until he learns to balance himself, he will run with short, energy-wasting strides. He will not run with the speed he will give you later when he has learned to shift his weight back and drive himself forward with his hindquarters.

Riding Alone

When you start going on trail rides alone, you will find that your horse is more likely to shy at roadside objects than when he was in the reassuring company of quiet horses. This stage will pass quickly unless, when he shies, you either 1. are caught by surprise and fall off, allowing the horse to run away in fright, or 2. react by pulling hard on the reins and gripping tightly with your legs, making him feel trapped, or 3. stop him and pat him. Any of the wrong reactions will encourage him to become "spooky."

If you are watchful, shying should not take you by surprise. I am sure you know by now how you should react to it. Make nothing of it. Keep the reins light, except for necessary checking and guidance, and ride on.

What should you do if you are riding alone and something beside the road frightens your horse so much that he refuses to go by it? Even though it is something that you know to be harmless, such as a pen full of sheep, you can hardly explain this verbally to the horse. The best thing to do is to dismount casually and lead the horse to the sheep pen, or to whatever object it is that terrifies him, taking as much time as necessary. Do not let him turn away from the object, but do not try to force him forward. Ask him forward step by step, allowing him to rest and evaluate the situation between steps, and he will gain confidence. (Do you remember using this technique when line-driving?) Once you have reached the object, stay there idly for at least five minutes, or until the horse has completely lost interest in it. Then remount and ride on.

Of course, you can try to *ride* your horse step by step toward an object that frightens him. It all depends on the degree of his fear. If he is almost panicky, he may experiment with tricks that you do not want him to learn, such as rearing and whirling. It is better to lead the horse to the object than to risk pressuring him into the discovery of a dangerous vice.

In the same way, use judgment if he hesitates at crossing a bridge. Try to ride him across it, but do not use force if he balks. Simply sit there, countering any attempt he makes to turn away. When he relaxes, ask him forward. If you do not succeed in inducing him to cross the bridge, dismount during a moment when he is relaxed, and lead him over it.

When you have had difficulties in passing by or crossing over certain obstacles on an outing, it is a good idea to double back over your trail on the way home, so that you can negotiate the same obstacles once again. The horse probably will not waste any time worrying about them on the return trip. He will remember that they resulted in no harm earlier, and he also will know that he is headed back to his stable.

Returning Home

It will be helpful during early training to plan your rides so that the most difficult obstacles are encountered on the way home.

When a young horse is fresh out of the stable he may be inclined to look for excuses to work off his excess energy. When he is heading homeward, he will be more interested in covering ground.

Although you can use the horse's homing instinct to advantage in training him to negotiate obstacles willingly, don't ever encourage or allow him to *hurry* back to his stable. When going for trail rides, remember the old saying: Always walk the first mile out and the last mile home. One reason for doing this is that it is advisable to warm a horse slowly to his work, and to cool him after work. Another reason is that a horse must learn to leave the stable quietly, and to return quietly. Whenever anyone complains that his horse always prances and frets on the way home, you can be sure that at some time or another he has allowed or urged the horse to gallop home. He may have done it only *one* time, but that is enough to generate a problem in a young horse.

After returning quietly from a cross-country ride, dismount at some place other than the entrance to the stable. Dismount before you arrive at the stable, or dismount in the stable yard, or ride past the stable and dismount. Don't let the horse get the idea that there is any special place for quitting work.

In your cross-country riding, your horse will become bolder as his confidence in you grows. Gradually, you can start increasing the challenges of terrain, to develop both boldness and agility. Ride up and down embankments, canter through woods, splash into streams at a trot. Of course, in doing this, you must consider the age and condition of the horse. The purpose of your riding is not to test his strength and endurance, but to promote his training.

Always go straight up or straight down steep inclines, and it will be easier for the horse to manage his balance. When going uphill, traveling straight, he can use the motive power of his hind legs to thrust his entire weight upward, and when going downhill, he can use his forelegs for support. Leave his head and neck free as he climbs or descends, but check him if he starts to hurry. To protect him from physical strain, and to instill discipline, he should be required to *walk* up and down steep inclines. If you feel that an incline is so steep that he cannot negotiate it without leaping and plunging, then bypass it.

Promoting Good Balance

By requiring the horse to restrain himself from picking up speed as he goes *down* steep inclines, you now will be introducing him to an important new signal. In order to keep himself from hurrying down the hill, *he will learn to shift his weight rearward in response to a check* on the reins. If you are capable of capitalizing on this, and can *gain control* of his balance on level ground through exercises that will be described shortly, you will be able to improve the quality of his gaits. You will be able to encourage him to move in good balance, with forehand lightened, and his awkwardness as a "green-broke" horse will begin to fade. He will be much more surefooted, and more comfortable to ride.

Actually, as a consequence of cross-country riding, the horse's gaits will show some improvement with little conscious assistance on your part. The horse will learn that when he is being ridden he is "going somewhere," instead of aimlessly circling as in an arena, and he will lose his early tendency to weave first one way and then another as he travels. And rough terrain will teach him to watch his footing, so he will voluntarily make adjustments in his balance and carriage in order to avoid stumbling. Well-read students of horsemanship know that Captain Vladimir S. Littauer, through his book *Common Sense Horsemanship*, has won a legion of followers who believe it is best for the average rider *not* to strive to *actively regulate* balance and collection in horses. He believes that relatively few riders have an aptitude for learning how to do it. Certainly, relatively few riders *do* learn how to do it, but whether it is because they lack the *aptitude* or the *desire* or simply the *opportunity* to learn how to do it is an open question.

If you have the desire to learn how to regulate the balance of your horse, the remainder of this chapter will give you the opportunity. You will note, however, that the subject is control of balance and not *collection*. Later, in more advanced training of your horse, you may want to teach him to respond to signals to collect himself—to gather himself like a compressed spring—so that he can move dynamically. At present, however, all you are asking of your horse is that he learn to move in good balance, so that he can turn and stop easily, and so he won't forge (step on his own feet) or be a stumbler.

It is natural for young horses to be heavy on the forehand when they are first ridden, particularly when they have been encouraged to accept riding calmly. In nature, when horses are calm, the bulk of their weight slumps forward. You can see by looking at them they are physically built to be heavy on the forehand. They can shift their balance rearward at will, simply by "leaning back" to transfer weight to their hind legs, and they do this when they want to move with agility. Since it requires greater expenditure of effort to move with hindquarters thus engaged for lift and drive than it does to move with weight slumped forward, free horses usually lean back and move lightly only for brief periods, most noticeably when they are excited.

If you want to teach your horse to be light on his feet under saddle, then it will be your task to teach and condition him to "carry himself from behind" at all times when being ridden. Regular cross-country riding will promote good balance only to a level that the horse finds adequate for his own purposes. He may learn to move well over tricky terrain, but succumb to boredom and become heavy on the forehand again when ridden on level roads or returned to the schooling arena.

Many good riders actively promote good balance in their horses without even thinking about it. They may not be able to explain it, but from past experience they know how it feels when a horse is heavy on the forehand, and how it feels when a horse shifts his weight back and uses or "engages" his hindquarters. They do it not only because it takes the roughness out of their horses' gaits, but because it improves maneuverability.

The little checking actions, which in dressage are called "half-halts," can be introduced to your horse as you ride down inclines, whether steep or gentle. It is less tiring to the horse and therefore more useful to work on gentle slopes. Find places where you can canter your horse up and down gently rolling terrain. Always start the cantering while going uphill. The canter will be smooth and comfortable as you go uphill, even on a green horse, because gravity keeps the horse's weight back. Concentrate on the way it feels.

As the horse tops the incline and starts to descend, if you do nothing to keep his balance back he will pitch forward and gain speed and the canter will become very rough. Don't let the horse's balance pitch forward. Use the reins to check his speed as necessary down the incline. You will know that you have succeeded in controlling his "leaning back while going forward" if the canter remains smooth, slow, and comfortable. When the ground levels, continue to use the checking action as you need it to remind the horse to remain light on the forehand. He may, at first, tend to misinterpret the checking as a signal to halt, so be prepared to use your legs as necessary to urge him to continue forward.

Don't expect the horse to grasp the point of the uphill-downhill exercise in one or two sessions. It will take time for him even to realize that you are teaching him a new signal.

The same exercise can be performed at the trot, but the canter is recommended for novice trainers because there is such a pronounced difference between success and failure. There is no mistaking a well-balanced canter—it invites the rider to sit down and be comfortable. Once a rider has learned to control a horse's balance at a canter, he can learn to do it at the trot and walk.

Another exercise for gaining control of the balance of a young horse consists of riding circles that gradually spiral inward and then outward. This exercise can be performed either in the countryside or in an arena. Again, it will be helpful to the novice trainer to do the work at the canter, although care must be taken not to fatigue the horse.

Why does circling encourage a horse to shift his balance rearward? *Because he cannot turn easily when he is heavy on the forehand.* If you start him on a circle about sixty feet in diameter, and gradually spiral inward to a circle about twenty feet in diameter, he will discover (through practice) that he must shift his weight rearward and engage the hindquarters to lift and drive himself into the direction of the diminishing circle. Until the horse makes the discovery that he can comply with your demands by engaging the hindquarters, it will seem to you that he is resisting the circling pattern. The smaller the circling, the more his hindquarters will tend to swing outward like the rear end of a motorcar that is allowed to coast instead of being driven around a curve. You can help him discover his balance by sitting deep in the saddle (don't lean forward) and by using a rhythmic checking action on the reins to coax him to lean back. You must keep both hands on the reins in order to help him with his balance as you guide him.

In doing this exercise, you can make it easy or difficult for the horse, depending upon the size of the circles you require. If the circles are too large, the exercise will not be challenging. If the circles become too small, before the horse has begun to find his balance, they will be too difficult, and will discourage him from even attempting to co-operate. Therefore, it is best to start on a large circle and then spiral inward gradually until you can feel that the horse is *beginning* to experience difficulty. At that point, the circle is small enough. Keep him on that circle, coaxing him to shift his balance rearward. As soon as he finds his balance, and moves easily around the circle, reward him by spiraling outward and bringing him to a walk. On the next try, you should be able to work your way inward to a smaller circle than before.

How can you tell when the horse is beginning to experience difficulty as he circles? You will know it, because he will start pulling against your turning hand. If you try to force him into an even smaller circle before he finds his balance, he either will stiffen his jaw and neck in desperate resistance against the turning, or he will start "rubbernecking." Do not force him into either of these defenses. If he learns one or the other, he will resort to it whenever he has difficulty in turning and will not learn to adjust his balance.

In any one schooling session, the circling exercise should be performed only briefly, just long enough to realize a little progress. However, it is necessary to work in both directions. You will find that the horse is more awkward with his balance when turning one way than the other, so allow a little more time for the "difficult side." It seems that horses, like people, have a natural inclination to be "right-handed" or "left-handed." This can be overcome with practice.

You may have heard that a rider is suppose to "bend" his horse into turns, using leg pressure to prevent the hindquarters from swinging outward. In early basic training, forget it. *That advice does not apply to horses that have not yet learned to engage the hindquarters.* A horse that is heavy on the forehand while turning is incapable of responding to a signal to hold his hindquarters to the track.

The object of the circling exercise is twofold. It develops the ability of the horse to move easily into turns, and, like the uphill-downhill exercise, it teaches him to lighten the forehand in answer to a checking action on the reins.

Unless the horse is tired, it is a good practice always to follow the circling exercise with some cantering on straight lines on level ground, encouraging the horse to remain light on the forehand. Again, your best clue to your success will be your own comfort in the saddle. The instant the horse starts to "spill forward" onto his forehand, his speed will increase and the gait will roughen. Try to keep him "back to hand," as the saying goes.

If you can, through the exercises described above, teach your horse to respond to the checking action and adjust his balance as you desire, people are going to think you have "magic" in your hands. Either that, or they are going to envy your "good fortune" in having found a young horse that moves so nicely.

If you cannot seem to get a feeling for controlling the balance of your horse, don't be discouraged. It may be that you are not ready for it now. It does not mean that you cannot still do a good job of giving your horse his basic training. Your alternative is simply to be patient and make liberal allowances for the fact that he is heavy on the forehand and moves awkwardly. Don't ask for quick turns and sudden halts. If you are careful never to try to force him to react beyond his capability, he will gradually become more and more capable.

Mechanical Gimmicks

It is no exaggeration to say that most riders do not understand the balance of their horses, and that most riders have pulling hands. When they try to force their poorly balanced horses to perform athletically, their pulling hands cause their horses to be high-headed, or low-headed, or stiff-necked, or rubber-necked, or hard-mouthed, or tender-mouthed. They blame the problems on their horses, not on themselves, and they try to overcome them with mechanical gimmicks. That is why saddlery shops enjoy a brisk business in martingales, draw reins, and unorthodox bits of all descriptions.

Skilled horsemen sometimes use martingales and other restraint devices, but they do not delude themselves that they are a cure for problems. They may use them on spoiled older horses that either are beyond retraining or are not worth retraining. Or they may use martingales on unspoiled horses as a precaution against accidental head-throwing when they are put to demanding work, such as calf-roping, jumping, or polo. However, they rarely use them when breaking young horses in to riding, because their ideal is to produce horses that work without mechanical gimmicks.

To see blatant examples of riders who ignorantly ask too much of their unbalanced horses, visit any of the gymkhana or "play-day" shows that are held across the country. In these shows, horses are ridden in contests requiring speed and agility—barrel races, flag races, keyhole races, and so forth. Unfortunately, many riders know more about speed than they do about agility. They can kick their horses into a run, but they do not know how to "set them up" for turns. And so they try to use brute strength to turn them. Then they wonder why their "stupid horses" throw their heads high and fight the turns. (Of course, some riders in gymkhanas know what they are doing, and it is a delight to watch them in action.)

To see *subtle* examples of riders who do not understand the balance of those horses, visit any of the dressage competitions held across the country. In these events, horses do not work at speed, and so their balance problems are less obvious. However, they are required to work in various degrees of collection, and the greater the degree of collection, the more the hindquarters must be engaged for lift and drive. Whenever you see a horse that appears to be leaning heavily on his rider's hands, or a horse that is moving with his head drawn back stiffly toward his rider, you can be certain that the rider does not know how to regulate the balance of the horse. As your eye sharpens, you will be astonished to note that some of the horses shown at the highest levels of dressage competition are ridden in poor balance.

In your work with your young horse, if head and mouth problems appear, don't disguise them with mechanical gimmicks. Accept them as a warning that you are asking too much of the horse at his level of training. Ease up on your demands, allow the horse to learn at his own rate, and the problems will disappear. Actually, there is very little chance that he will develop any such problems during his basic training if you leave the reins long enough for him to carry his head and neck in a natural position, and use resisting instead of pulling hands to direct him.

As the horse gains experience under saddle, his responses to your signals will become a matter of habit, and you can ride him with increasing subtlety. Make a conscious effort to "lighten" your signals and make them less and less conspicuous. Keep both hands low and close to the horse. Don't move one hand sideways to lead the horse through a turn unless he needs it.

Neck-Reining

If you want to teach your horse to neck-rein so that you can ride him with one hand, simply start routinely applying a neck-rein in conjunction with his normal signal to turn. Be careful not to pull the horse's nose to the outside with the neck-reining hand, or he will not be able to look into the turn. Over a period of several weeks, the horse gradually will learn to respond to the neck-rein alone.

After that, you can ride with one hand, so long as you do not ask the horse to make turns that require a decided change of balance. Even if you know how to help the horse with his balance, it takes two hands to control the balance of a *green* horse. (In more advanced training, the horse eventually learns to respond to signals from the rider's seat for balance control.)

At any time now, you can start teaching the horse a slower trot. It is good for a horse to learn at least two "speeds" at the trot. The slow trot, whether it is the shifty little jog of the Western horse, or the so-called "sitting trot" of the hunter hack, is comfortable to ride, and will be important later if you start schooling for extension and collection.

If you can control the horse's balance, you will have little difficulty in bringing him back to a slower trot and settling him into it. If you cannot, use circling figures and gentle, uphill inclines to slow him. It may be several days or weeks before he "catches on" to the new speed at the trot, but one day he will surprise you by finding and holding it as though it's no trouble at all.

Reining Back

How about teaching the horse to rein back? Backing has not been mentioned earlier because it is unwise to introduce it to a young horse before he has been conditioned to respond willingly to signals to go forward. Also, it is easier to teach a horse to rein back after he has learned something about his balance under a rider.

I am always amused at "experts" who introduce the subject of backing by saying that it is "very hard for horses because it is not natural to them to walk backward," as though a physical problem were involved. It is no more difficult for horses to walk backward than it is for people to walk backward. One reason horses tend to resist it at first, and one reason that they would like to turn their heads or twist sideways as they do it, probably has something to do with the fact that they cannot see where they are going. (Is it natural for *you* to walk backward without wanting to look over your shoulder?) However, the main reason that so many horses develop problems about backing has nothing to do with any natural reluctance to do it. The main reason is that so many riders have pulling hands. A horse cannot be taught to rein back smoothly and easily by a rider who tries to pull him backward.

To teach your horse to rein back, remember that you must not pull. You must induce him to step backward voluntarily. How can you do it? In the same way that you taught him to reduce pace without pulling.

If you are using a bit, apply a little pressure to his mouth, and then maintain the pressure with a fixed hand. There should be just enough pressure to make the horse slightly uneasy, but not enough to bring his nose in toward his chest. The horse will start experimenting with ways to find relief from the discomfort. He may try tugging against your hands. If he does, resist the tugging, and maintain the pressure. He may try dipping his nose in toward his chest. If he does, use a short and swift lifting action on one rein to raise the head and get the nose out, then restore the pressure instantly. Finally, the horse will try stepping backward. Release the pressure simultaneously, as his reward. One step backward is all you need in the first lesson. Ride him forward, and give him a pat.

Always ride forward immediately after backing, so that the horse will learn to expect it, and thus will have an incentive to keep his legs well under him. Otherwise, he might develop a tendency to move backward in a sprawling manner. Don't be in a hurry to multiply the number of steps that he takes backward. For several days, at least, ask only for one or two steps at a time, and start forward while he is going well. As he develops confidence, he will offer more and more steps back. You will find that, once he has started backward, he will take successive steps more readily if you give and take with one rein rather than both.

If you are using a bosal, do not apply and maintain a fixed pressure to induce him to start backward. Take a *light* feel of his nose with the bosal, and then with one hand start a gentle "bumping" action against his nose with the bosal. If he dips his nose toward his chest, use the short lifting action to raise the head, and continue the bumping until it occurs to him to step backward to escape it.

The rider should use only his hands, and not his legs, in teaching a young horse to rein back. It is only in more advanced training that the legs can be used without confusing the horse. It is important now to keep everything simple.

When a horse backs correctly, he does not change his posture. His head and neck remain in a natural position. He moves straight, and *his legs move in diagonal pairs*. If his legs move one at a time, as when walking forward, he will not be well balanced, and will not travel smoothly.

If the horse shows an inclination to swing his hindquarters to one side as he reins back, then practice alongside a fence or a wall. Once he has learned to step backward correctly, he will no longer need the wall as a "crutch."

What more should your horse learn in the course of his basic training?

There are no standards or rules that define the limits of basic training. In my opinion, a horse's basic training is complete when he is an experienced and trustworthy "pleasure" horse or hack. If you want to ride your horse in pleasure classes in horse shows, it would be well to teach him to take up the canter from the walk (if he is a Western or Saddle horse), or from the slow trot (if he is a hunter). You can teach him a simple "cue" for his leads. The simplest is this: An instant before asking for a canter depart, check him and turn him slightly *away* from the direction of movement. Then ask for the canter, simultaneously turning him *into* the direction of movement. In doing this, you are *creating a turn* that naturally encourages the correct lead. If you wish, you can accompany this maneuver with a "leg cue," and the horse eventually will learn to take his leads from the leg cue alone. A little pressure of your *right* leg behind the girth should become the signal for the *left* lead, and vice versa. These signals are widely used by riders in horse shows, and they bear a primitive but distinct relationship to the signals that will be used in more advanced training.

Even though the training outlined in this book has been described as basic training, if you have accomplished it with your horse you now have an exceptional mount. He is not schooled in any specialties that require him to move like an athlete, but he is a joy to handle and to ride, and it is no exaggeration to say that it is all to your credit.

It might seem, in the reading of this book, that you should never be around your horse except when you are training him. If it does, it is because whenever you are with him you *are* training him. Every time you groom him you are training him. Every time you mount him you are training him. Every time you go riding with friends on the trail, you are training him. He is influenced, for better or for worse, by every contact he has with you, or with anyone else. If you don't believe this, let a friend take care of him and ride him for a week. If the friend is a better horseman than you, then you will be surprised at the improvement in your horse's way of going under saddle. If the friend is a poor horseman, then you will be dismayed at problems that have appeared, both in your horse's ground manners and in his behavior when you ride him.

This does not mean, however, that being with your horse is all work and no play, and that your attitude toward the horse should be detached and clinical. Far from it. It does mean that because you understand your horse he will come to understand you, and this will generate a special bond between you.

I think the greatest compliment I ever received as a horseman came from a child I taught for several years. We were discussing what it would be like to be a horse. I said, "When I see how most people handle their horses, I am convinced I would never want to be one." The child looked thoughtful. "Well," she said, "I wouldn't mind being a horse . . . if I could be yours."